Thinkers
AND SINKERS ™

"Why Are They Trying To Kill You?"

Thinkers AND SINKERS™

"Why Are They Trying To Kill You?"

Davida Patrick Moore

Many Moore Designs

©2011 Many Moore Designs

First Edition 2011

ISBN 978-0-615-45040-7

All graphics and illustrations by Davida Patrick Moore
Photos by Blanka Kielb

**See audio book offer on page 248.
or visit: ThinkersAndSinkers.com/tsaudio**

Dedication

To those who yearn to learn
that which they do not know
and those who strive
for greater comprehension
of what they have already
begun to understand.

Reading Suggestions
Please Read

This book is presented having reading options for various ways in which to approach the contents. To access the information use each part separately and/or together.

Begin with the, "Skimming the Surface," portions. Here a reader can quickly access essential concepts in the material. These thoughts can be pondered individually. The chapter and verse numbers need not be read yet correlate to a broader expression within the subsequent portions.

Next the, "Entering the Waters," paragraphs are presented. Here a few sentences layout the general framework of the concept to be explored with greater detail in the proceeding section. **Reading these portions first is a great way to whet the inquisitive mind for this discussion at hand.**

And finally the, "Deeper Depths," segments of the manuscript - here the reader is offered finer illustrations of the concepts. This portion of the book is most of all for study. The concepts are interconnected with other parts of the book and in detail underpin the intricate construction of the thesis that is this book.

For quicker access and recaps, simply read the posters that appear at the end of chapters; 1, 3, 11, 14, and 20, and then review the lists of Thinker and Sinker traits that appear between chapters 9 and 10. From all the options discover how you can best explore the information.

At the end of the book the reader will find a, "Concordance." Here the reader can explore the manuscript noting where specific words are mentioned.

Reading separate chapters will impart useful information yet it is suggested that the material be read in the order presented. It is also suggested that the whole manuscript be studied over time to seat the concepts in the conscious and subconscious portions of the mind. Here the greatest ability of activating the uplifting, Thinker, mindset can be engaged to the benefit of the individual.

Take note of the, "audio track," numbers that appear at the head of each segment or feature. These track numbers correlate to the complete, "word-for-word," recorded version of this book.

An audio book offer can be found on page 248 or by visiting: ThinkersAndSinkers.com/tsaudio.

Acknowledgments

The writing of this book has been propelled by a bountiful list of inspiring and supportive individuals, as well as, countless herd members. To begin, I wish to acknowledge and thank my parents and siblings for their generous spiritual and material support. Acquiring the time to bring this book to fruition is due in large part to them. The lessons they illustrated, knowingly and unknowingly, proved their worth in these pages.

My longtime friend and endless inspirer, Renée Mulcahy along with her husband Mike have my gratitude. Renée for being who she is, an Everlasting Star, and Mike for his strength and his supporting of his wife. Brian Sisson's intellect and flawless sounding board attributes were beyond value to me in the process of writing this book. My deepest thanks and appreciation goes out to each of them.

Those who do not know of their contributions to this book are all the uplifting examples throughout the ages and most readily those who are currently acting to inspire.

Who cannot be overlooked are all those judgmental, egocentric, and destructive personalities. By their actions we are all able to better see the folly of the Sinker mindset. I am perpetually grateful for their ill-behavior as they give me renewed and daily examples of the behavior this book is meant to illustrate. With their continued pursuit of destruction the needed lessons are refreshed. In time, they will gather in these lessons and discover for themselves how to be their most uplifting and loving selves.

Those who read the early versions of this book and those who were unable to get through them, I appreciate all your efforts and feedback. No action or inaction went unnoticed and I am heartened by it all.

And lastly, I acknowledge the importance of the times we live in and the extraordinary fortune of which we find ourselves the recipients. To the amazing source of our creation I humbly say, "Thank you, thank you, thank you."

Thanks for reading and thinking.

Davida Patrick Moore

Table of Contents

Prologue
(Skimming the Surface)

00:01 As we act, we promote the choosing
of the high road or the low road.

00:02 Through thoughtful reflection, an
alternative to judgment can be found.

00:03 There will always be opinions and concepts that
one may find untrue, undesirable, or unfathomable.

00:04 Every person can be
accepting and judgmental.

00:05 The supreme good is
something to aspire to.

00:06 When needed, nothing can take the
place of good psychiatric care.

00:07 Knowing the meaning of
every word is important.

00:08 We have the option to acknowledge
we are all challenged in some way.

00:09 There are people, wielding influence,
that seek to shape how others act.

Prologue
(Entering the Waters)

- With free will, the experience of humanity is jostled by the choices of being accepting or judgmental (the Thinker and the Sinker).

- Naturally, humankind seeks expansion yet paradoxically humankind can succumb to fear of the unknown.

- Ordinarily, a person can identify positive events and we have names for the source of those events.

- The laws of cities, states, and nations will change. The Laws of Nature do not.

- Understanding the words, motivations, and goals of a person, country, or ideology is to understand what influences them.

- When someone understands love they become a minister of love. If we choose other than love we neglect love. When we neglect love, we do not choose life . . . and will surely perish.

Prologue
(Deeper Depths)

00:01 **The most meaningful summons ever received by humankind is illustrated in the metaphor of Thinkers and Sinkers.** The Thinker mindset is found in those who hear the call to be accepting and considerate of others. They rise in their experience of life. The Sinker mindset is revealed in those who feel persuaded to be judgmental and are feeling of a need to manipulate others. In life, this leads to the sinking into the depths of loss and despair. The importance of this discourse is found in the fact that each trait is constantly acting upon the whole of humanity in opposite directions, up with the Thinker, and down with the Sinker. At any given moment, how we think and act will promote the success of one and not the other.

00:02 **A Thinker would likely say:** "Trying to control you, the Sinker actually hopes to transform themselves. This is their thought process. We want them to understand that we know they think they need to spiritually and/or physically kill to assuage their own perceived shortcomings. We hope this will make them think deeply as to what they are actually trying to do in this world. If sufficiently reflected upon, they will learn to live for themselves and truly become what they desire: **self-aware**, **self-dependent**, and **self-realized**. In a word they will become . . . **FREE**."

00:03 The above paragraph is describing the conflict between worldviews held on some level by all humans on the planet earth. What follows is a dissection of this thesis. In the delineation, concepts are offered which may, at first, appear unreal. Yet it is the fervent belief of the author that with open discussion, honesty, and self-acceptance each person will find a reasonable understanding of where they are currently centered in the spectrum of human awareness and how that relates to the difficulties of understanding and accepting some concepts. This information is shared from a spiritual disposition. Those looking for academic rigor are asked to fully consider the material with their heart.

00:04 At this time, human nature, and every individual, possesses traits of both the Thinker and the Sinker. Determining how much of each is challenging, yet will potentially portend the trending in one's life experience. If we seek to understand ourselves and others we display, and can then develop, our loving and accepting, Thinker nature. If we discard this exploration we reveal a potentially egocentric and judgmental, Sinker nature. The Thinker is in line with the higher ideals of Truth, Wisdom, and Bliss. The Sinker is rooted in ego, wants, and domination. Where these traits lead are to opposing realities of, ultimate fulfillment (the Thinker), and utter destruction (the Sinker). Yet, if enough people gain clarity on the **psychology** and **extenuating motivations** forming each persuasion more people will learn to navigate life. With their behavior these individuals will then serve as uplifting examples to others.

00:05 Every so often in this book the discussion will include the concept of a, **"Supreme Good,"** that thing people call, "GOD." This is a reference to the ultimate good (whatever that might mean to the reader). Divinity is a word used to express our connection to that good. As you read, you can note that emphasis, and the absolute displacement of even the slightest judgment. The Supreme Good is thought by many to be the origin of our existence but not likely a personage as so many understand from classic references to GOD. We will leave that discussion for a later date. In this book different words will be used for this thing. The reader will likely recognize them as such. In this book, there are no requirements for any religious observations. The mission in this book is to prompt people to think about how they think regarding themselves, others, and the conditions supporting a state of supreme goodness. The reason for this mission is to aid in accepting and supporting the unique and Divine gift that is each and every person living today and those to come in the future.

00:06 **"Thinkers and Sinkers,"** is not intended to take the place of the appropriate assistance for those who are in need of counseling or psychiatric care. It is intended for those who wish to be honest with themselves and can thoughtfully explore and express what and how they think regarding their belief system and the concepts found in these pages. This book contains opinions and extrapolations of concepts that in some light make sense. No one is telling, or being told, what, and what not to do. Observations are offered that are believed to be true. Suggestions are made that are believed to be for the most good. The word, "must," is used to reflect the author's perspective and is not intended to indicate absolutes imposed upon the reader. The contents of this book are meant as thoughts to be contemplated. The author wholeheartedly embraces the reality that everyone will do in life as they desire.

00:07 The **importance of language** is highly regarded by the author. The words used in this book are so employed to elicit a particular mental image. If you do not fully understand a word or have any question as to its meaning please research the word so the fullest meaning can be obtained. Please forgive the author if this suggestion finds you put off in any way.

00:08 This book was written to earnestly express what is understood regarding choices we make in ascending and descending upon **Jacob's Ladder**. Those choices are wrapped by a protective sheath and found at our very core. At our core is **The Power To Love**, the option to accept what we find difficult and to allow others to have their experience; to be available for those we can; to acknowledge the challenges we all have; to protect ourselves physically and emotionally; to shed the outgrown burden of herd mentality and release the unique gift in each of us; to reconcile ourselves to the unknown, giving credence to something greater than ourselves.

00:09 How we see the world around us and how we choose to respond to that world determines what our life means to us and directs what our world will become in the future. Yet the perspective from which we work has been influenced by a long and growing list of sources. Our minds are powerful. Yet when freed into a loving way, our hearts are indomitable. We are called to forever discern the information that is imparted to us. Otherwise, we end up blindly following those directing us. Do some people want others to simply do as they are told? Is it human nature to want our opinions to be largely accepted? Are we truly here to live a life of joy? The answers to those questions are: yes, yes, and yes. How we perceive those questions and how we respond to what they represent is definitive. But the success of our lives and the ultimate happiness of every soul is first attached to the endeavor of living a life.

Introduction
(Skimming the Surface)

00:10 In an emotional sense, what we
experience can lift us up or pull us down.

00:11 Happy or sad, people will often
want others to feel like them.

00:12 When focused on life we can see, hear, and
feel, unconditional love, truth, wisdom, and bliss.

00:13 There will always be opinions and
concepts that some will disagree with.

00:14 One's focus can add energy to
the desirable and the undesirable.

00:15 Every person possesses traits
reflecting acceptance and judgment.

00:16 It is beneficial to accept that
we are human, imperfect yet capable.

00:17 How we act is up to us.

Introduction
(Entering the Waters)

- There are influences in life that lift us up and there are influences that try to pull us down.

- People enjoy like-minded company.

- As we live life we culture ourselves by what we think, believe, and do. Continuously we react to what we perceive and conceive. This develops our character.

- If we are open to circumstances and possibilities we reflect the Thinker mindset and we rise.

- If we respond with judgment and a closed heart we display the Sinker mindset, lowering ourselves into loss and despair.

- There are no mistakes, yet every action has a consequence. The consequences we experience are chosen, by us, in our thoughts and actions.

Introduction
(Deeper Depths)

00:10 In an emotional sense, what we experience in life **can buoy us** or **pull us down**. A person's life experience can be seen as a collection of thoughts and actions. In those thoughts and actions a plethora of emotions, experiences, and extenuating circumstances blossom, bringing forth more of these events.

00:11 **Happy people** want others to be happy. Those who feel pulled down will often attempt anything to stop the feelings of their downward trend, if even only superficially. Engaging, and if need be, overcoming one's life situation is largely possible, if desired. This is done as a factor of one's **personality, characteristics**, and **motivation.**

00:12 We are all on our way somewhere. How we get there is of our design, however odd or unfounded, opinionated or grand. Yet in our going we either choose our goal by intellect or the route is dictated through instinct. As we do this, the design of our **Creative Source** is forever communicated to us. When attuned to witness life we see, hear, and feel, unconditional love, truth, wisdom, and bliss. If we choose to accept these offerings we choose to accept specific Divine guidance. To evidence this directive we must open our hearts to love.

00:13 We all do things that others would not. We believe in things that others do not. We hold concepts that motivate us which show signs of being imprecise in the vast analysis of the grand design. But that is what makes us human and makes our experience unique.

00:14 In life there will be objects, situations, and behaviors that one will find desirable and undesirable. These circumstances will appear and will call for a response. If we dwell on the undesired, our **energy** is directed toward that object, situation, or behavior. When **energy** and effort is focused on something that is undesirable that same **energy** and effort cannot be channeled into something desirable. Focusing on the undesirable can convert the observer to the **energetic level** of the undesired object, situation, or behavior. This is often a goal of the destructive. With loving intent, the observer can create something uplifting by which to displace the undesired object, situation, or behavior. This positive response is constructive.

00:15   Every person possesses traits reflecting **acceptance** and **judgment**. As we repeatedly engage one, the other recedes. Yet we are more one than the other. In this we can be thought of as Thinkers or Sinkers, the capable or less-capable swimmer in the proverbial **River of Life**. The questions are, how well of a Thinker and how much of a Sinker.

00:16   Here, we see we are all together. Yet by the Source of our creation nothing is **expected**, nothing **demanded**, and nothing is **disallowed**. Here, we concede to being human and know we will make it through this experience. We continue our existence from where we will, fully aware that, while we are here, we choose our response to everything we encounter.

00:17   Who we allow ourselves to be is our **choice**.

Chapter 1
Where We Are
(Skimming the Surface)

01:01 Every life is lived solely by the individual.

01:02 Beyond the individual there is family, nationality, culture, ideology, and so on.

01:03 The last and largest group one can belong to is either mostly accepting or mostly judgmental.

01:04 As individuals, who we are is based more in thoughts or feelings.

01:05 With love a person can have an expansive and uplifting life.

01:06 Everything changes.

01:07 A level of achievement can inspire and lead to more achievement.

01:08 Acceptors seek balance knowing it will not be permanent.

01:09 The balance point between acceptance and judgment is always changing.

01:10 Everyday new things happen
showing us how others live.

01:11 If two people disagree one is
more correct than the other.

01:12 In time everyone can
find some success.

01:13 An acceptor is like an abled swimmer;
the judgmental is like a less-abled swimmer.

01:14 Everyone wants their way, either
to be helpful or to soothe their feelings.

01:15 Propaganda can easily
mislead those who are careless.

01:16 Humankind is here to grow in
understanding and awareness of itself.

01:17 Everyone has a purpose and
the ability to fulfill that purpose.

Chapter 1

Where We Are
(Entering the Waters)

- People are unique, each with a personality containing some measure and form of reason and emotion.

- How we recognize our personal reason and emotions and how we respond to these thoughts refines our personality.

- One's personality can be uplifting or a weight, pulling one's self and others down in spirit.

- An uplifting life is about possibilities and the development of capabilities. These people are mostly of the, "Thinker," mindset. The downward spirit is judgmental of one's self and others and is found in the, "Sinker," mindset.

- Because we are here, we are called upon to live a life.

- We can choose to be accepting and loving, matching the Thinker mindset, or we can choose to be judgmental and cruel, matching the Sinker mindset.

- Matching our conscious and unconscious choices, the events of our lives will follow the prevailing direction of the mindset we embrace. This is us creating and directing the course of our life experience.

Chapter 1
Where We Are
(Deeper Depths)

**One Wishes To Become The Other.
The Other Wishes To Be Themselves.**

Niels Bohr a physicist and quantum mechanic is attributed to have said, "The opposite of a correct statement is a false statement. But the opposite of a profound truth may well be another profound truth." This quote shows that in profound matters perspective is integral.

01:01 Amongst all the **variables** in this world, perspective is the greatest in the ability to produce unique reasoning and emotions. We alone, as individuals, witness first hand the totality of our life. From our station, in the ever-evolving mass that is humanity, we live a singularly unique life. While some aspects may match the experience of others, at the level of the individual there are no **duplicates**. There is Divine and Cosmic purpose in our being unique and individual. As you continue reading this will become clear.

01:02 Rising above our individuality we see that we are a part of a family, however connected or disconnected. We have ancestral lineage. Above the level of the **family** we become part of a **community**, however we define that. As we rise further we recognize **nationality**, **culture**, and **ideology** as larger groups to which we may count ourselves.

01:03 At the very top of this structure we will fundamentally reveal ourselves as belonging more to one of two competing perspectives. These two perspectives are composed of thoughts and actions that define each perspective - one is **accepting**, the other **judgmental**. These two halves seek to take the population of the world in different directions - one is very loving, one is less so.

01:04   One perspective is predicated more on **reason** and the other more on **emotion**. The greatest benefit would be found if both truly understood their own perspective and that of their counterpart. For one it is less of a challenge to do so.

01:05   The acceptor works to improve their experience and by extension that of those around them. They seek to, "rise." **Rising** is a spiritual/metaphysical term that relates to a natural and holistic communion with nature, the source of our origin and purpose. In a person this nature provides the capacity to witness the uplifting aspects of situations, events, and interactions within this life. The expansion one experiences during an **epiphany** is comparable to this rising process. In this life one is either rising or **sinking**.

01:06   The one thing we can count on in this life is change. Everything changes. It may seem that some things do not change but they do. No one stays unchanged. No one stays at the same emotional or intellectual level in life forever. A person will feel differently, think differently, and respond differently at different times in their life. However slight the movement, one can be assured change is forever occurring.

01:07   As one rises and reflects upon their interpretation of others who may not have risen as much, one can look back to assess their own growth. In this reflection one can consider ways to inspire those seeking to rise as they pursue life. For a person who has risen, in a matter of speaking, looking down reveals from where they came. Those who have not risen well can look down yet this only re-enforces what they seek to rise out of.

01:08   Those who have yet to rise much can look up but have little way to intensely connect with what they see. Those who have risen continue in the fashion they have developed, to rise as they might. In their acceptance they trust in their actions and believe, as acceptors do, in the greatness of their endeavor and the promise of possibilities. They understand that **balance** in this life will never be permanently attained yet in their accepting they are content to believe that balance can always be sought. Positions possessing greater balance hold more opportunity for choice. Events are more often dictated in positions with less balance. In achieving balance between these competing philosophies, however brief, benefits will come from reflection and acceptance. For one it will be less of a challenge to do so.

01:09 When one philosophy has too great of influence, balance is lost. Much like the sphere that is the earth the balancing of humanity is also attempted on a sphere, a sphere of consciousness, a sphere of beliefs, perspectives, and of willingness. This sphere consist of all perspectives. This does not mean that the balance point between the two parties is static. As time passes the sphere upon which we are poised rolls forward and upward. In a matter of speaking this is the path of our **growth** and **evolution**. The balance point between the two philosophies will likely change endlessly.

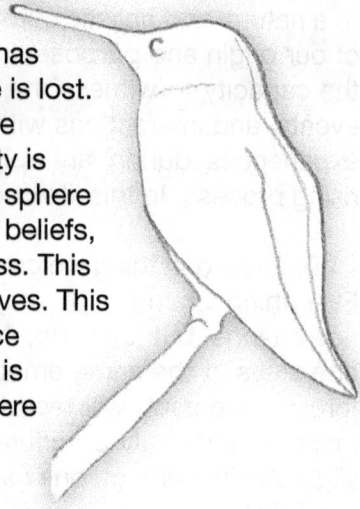

01:10 Everyday new experiences occur to add expanded dimension to our personal lives and our collective experience on a multitude of levels. As communication becomes farther-reaching and the time lag from event to report grows shorter, we become more connected to each other. From our perspectives we witness more of the lives others experience. This leads to the sharpening of our awareness of what is different and similar between us.

01:11 Between the two philosophies, one will always have a greater understanding of a specific situation and the necessities needed to achieve a longer-lasting structure within that situation.

01:12 An acceptor is not guaranteed success in all endeavors. Even someone judgmental has possibilities for success. Though statistically the two will not split 50-50 the total productive ideas to be had. While one philosophy, if left in charge without opposition, would have more positive solutions to a vital debate, the other party would not. Determining which is which is a major conflict in the public domain.

01:13 Of these two philosophies, one is akin to a **capable swimmer** and the other to a **less-capable swimmer**. One will more likely keep their head above water, the other will very possibly not. It is not known if someone cannot swim until they have proven the fact by drowning. The pursuits of these swimmers will return results that are somewhat equivalent to their capabilities. For the less-capable swimmer this will persist in some fashion as or until they learn to adequately swim, drown, or are assisted by another in keeping their head above the water.

01:14 Being that if people, accepting or judgmental, have consciousness, and holding fast to their beliefs, they will likely seek to further their viewpoints; **rhetorically** and **actually**. Both sides will seek adherents in an attempt to gain influence and thereby bolster their position, lending credibility to their desired direction. This is done to positively impact society or to assuage their personal feelings of shortcomings. These adherents might be found through public opinion. The credibility sought might be found in authoritative rule.

01:15 If humanity is not thoughtful it will be more easily affected by controlling and **deleterious** propaganda. But even through this propaganda the true motives can be seen. The Righteousness of the most fundamental ideals are immutable while the propaganda drums must be pounded on a daily basis as to not allow divergent thoughts to penetrate the consciousness of the propagandist's target. This reveals that the manipulative, hopeless, and judgmental Sinker philosophy is, in a matter of speaking, trying to spiritually and/or physically kill, others and themselves. Understanding why will help to displace the efforts they employ.

01:16 We are on this planet to express ourselves. If we do this in a loving way we will rise. In that experience we will evolve in our understanding and awareness of our origin, abilities, potential, and purpose. There will be those who are lacking in their personal connection to this awareness yet they are capable of expansion if they apply the innate faculty that, on this planet, is uniquely human. This faculty encompasses acceptance and **The Power To Love**.

01:17 Every person on this planet is summoned to this role and each can approach the endeavor. As they do, it will be in their own way. What motivates, influences, and distracts us as individuals is where we encounter our own personal experience. **This is how we live our lives.**

Chapter 1 - Where We Are

"**Have courage,**" can sound an ominous undertone.

If told, "the only thing we have to fear, is **fear itself**," we have been told to be fearful. If we allow ourselves to fear fear we become that which we hoped to overcome.

The lure that draws so many to the Sinker mentality poses to allay our slightest inkling of discomfort. In fending off the discomfort the lure deflects its own work made to draw the unaware to the Sinker's sphere of influence and plan for the target's **ultimate demise**. This reveals the complexity and the relentless mindset of the Sinker mentality.

The ego that creates a problem so it may resolve the same, shows the **unbalanced** mindset of the Sinker.

Chapter 2

Concepts and Perspectives
(Skimming the Surface)

02:01 Ideas, and how we look at those ideas,
play a big part in what motivates us.

02:02 Understanding the differences between instinct,
intuition, inspiration, and intelligence is vital.

02:03 Beyond the five senses
information is communicated.

02:04 Perceptions beyond the five
senses cannot be fully discounted.

02:05 What is done with information
can be more important than the information.

02:06 A person's focus can
change a moment and a life.

02:07 Intelligence is not fool proof.

02:08 Reasoning can be manipulated.

02:09 The potential factors that can
influence our behavior are many.

02:10 One will benefit from considering
the process of how they think.

02:11 Continuously refining one's
thought process is valuable.

02:12 Writing is a great way to
more fully form ideas one holds.

02:13 Understanding how and why
we act can guide us toward wisdom.

02:14 It is as important to know why
one thinks as it is what one thinks.

02:15 Beliefs can reveal one's own human
weaknesses, potential, and purpose.

02:16 Openly discussing life circumstances
with valued counsel can prevent unfounded
acceptance of the beliefs of others.

Chapter 2
Concepts and Perspectives
(Entering the Waters)

- It is extremely important to be conscious of the ideas we have, where these ideas come from, and to where they lead.

- Where we put our focus is from where our experience is created.

- Influential factors are everywhere.

- If we do not pay attention to our thoughts we give our lives over to our instincts.

- Knowing why we think what we think can reveal our thought process.

- Every belief we hold must be available for scrutiny. Is a life unexamined worth living?

Chapter 2
Concepts and Perspectives
(Deeper Depths)

02:01 Ideas, and how we look at those ideas, play a monumental role in how we are motivated in life. How we perceive the concepts presented us will shape how we interact in the future with people, situations, and events. We rely on what we have observed along with what we have been told, and taught, for **decision-making**, however accurate. Intuition is another source that motivates our actions. Although it is not ranked as a sense, humans have long used intuition in decision-making. Yet how one interprets their intuition can potentially guide or misguide.

02:02 To many, the blurry line between intuition and the five senses is an acceptable argument for overlooking the importance of intuition. This does not dissuade those who have developed their intuition to a heightened level. For absolute clarity it must be stated, inspiration and intuition are two entirely different things. Inspiration comes from outside the human body. Intuition comes from within the human body. Intuitive answers to questions ought not be rejected without consideration. Understanding the differences between inspiration, intuition, and instinct is vital.

02:03 **Instinct** is knowingness without conscious thought. **Intuition** is self-direction that leads one to a conclusion without precise details and has been considered to be a kind of sixth sense. Other forms of sixth sense are clairvoyance "clear seeing," clairaudient "clear hearing," clairsentient "clear feeling," and others. **Inspiration** is a concept that appears in one's mind nearly, if not completely, formed.

02:04 The idea of a **sixth sense** is widely understood in the Western world. This sixth sense could be compared to the gift of prophecy recorded since ancient times. For this discussion we will depart from talk of extra-sensory perception. But we cannot fully discount extra sensory perception, intuition, feelings, and emotions. Although they can be manipulated and self-diverting, for many they are unquestionably present. For this discussion we will concentrate on the spoken and written word keeping an almost unmentioned shadow of intuition in the background.

02:05   What we do with the information we receive regarding the world around us is sometimes more important than the information. Perception changes everything. Two people, side-by-side, can view and interpret the same information in completely different ways. How one applies their **logic** or succumbs to their **emotional needs** will determine much.

02:06   What a person chooses to question, or not, can reveal a momentary mood or their worldview. At any moment a person could be thoughtfully engaged in their surroundings and the events that they perceive as affecting their life, or be not so involved.

02:07   Lastly, we need to consider intelligence. The importance of **intelligence** cannot be overstated yet is not fool proof either. Everyone has a blind spot and people who are thought to be intelligent are no different. The ability to reason is a sign of intelligence yet sometimes reason is not as useful as faith or intuition.

02:08   Intelligence is the ability to acquire and apply knowledge. Determining if information is factual is very important but not strictly a matter of anything called **knowledge**. Someone's intelligence can be used against him or her to elicit a desired response. Reasoning can be manipulated where an otherwise intelligent individual buys into fallacies such as: straw man, slippery slope, argumentum ad hominem, and relativist fallacies. What passes for intelligence can actually be a handle by which someone can be guided or manipulated.

02:09   The potential factors that can influence our behavior run the gamut of; intelligence, or the lack there of, emotional state of mind, quality of reasoning possessed, interest in the subject, the framing of the information, the perceived validity of the information, the delivery form of the information, and the shadow of instinct and intuition.

02:10 To have a more complete overview one might consider their process and think about how they think. Instead of simply running through the day doing the chores they have assigned themselves, recognizing opportunities, and remembering events, faces, and obligations, there is an often forgotten process of refining one's consciousness, awareness, and intellect. This can be done through a process that includes **deep reflection**.

02:11 Thinking about how one thinks is similar to recognizing when knowledge is being employed. In different fields of study, the term **Metacognition** is used differently yet the term is useful here. For this discussion we will apply the accepted definition of, "knowing how one thinks," and "recognizing the process of learning." Refining our thought process through Metacognition is desirable.

02:12 Writing is a great way of more fully forming the ideas one holds. Fleshing out concepts on paper demands more thorough thought. Researching the work and experience of others can lend valuable perspective to one's own endeavors. Weighing the opinions and discerned findings of another is worthy. How well one performs this exercise will potentially be rewarded by more thoughtful beliefs. Well thought out, if not well founded beliefs attract similar energy (read; consciousness).

02:13 Those who go along to get along may be swept into an uplifting behavior, yet without greater understanding of the activity a less-fulfilling involvement may result. Then there are those that are thoughtless as to their involvement in a mindset who, only after time, discover the unsettling direction of their behavior.

02:14 Why one thinks what they think is as important as the beliefs they hold. This is because the influence of the belief will lead to other behaviors that will form the individual's life experience. Caring, as well as one can, to understand a belief one holds is to care for one's self. To more fully understand a belief, one would have given the subject much consideration and could speak on the subject at length.

02:15 Exposing one's motives for a deeply held belief opens that person up to discover potential revelations of their own **frailties**. If we flee from our frailties we surrender the greatness our life can attain - the purpose for our being. If we retreat from admissions of our humanity we simply become animated objects and lessen our potential. Even if we start by admitting only to ourselves we begin to face the shortcomings we recognize as not contributing the positive achievements we can. Once we start we can displace concepts we adhered to for the perceived benefits, which in the end do not uplift us.

02:16 **Confession** is a remedy of great value when it comes to unburdening the heart. Openly discussing personal behavior and emotions with respected and experienced counsel is a valuable attribute of humanity. We are not alone in our frailties. Acknowledging our need for understanding and comfort in times of uncertainty shows our evolved self. Though airing our thoughts is of value it is not as important as disengaging what we perceive as lacking behavior. Actions speak louder than words. People live lives suppressed by beliefs they hold so as to be a part of a structure they blindly accept. Often these concepts are formulated outside of them, by the Sinker mentality, to manipulate them into the role of follower as opposed to accepting them in the role of an inspirer. Discarding undesirable behavior is more than suppressing the influence but truly displacing it from the conscious and subconscious mind. Everyone has a role in this life that is uplifting.

Uncovering that role can be done most easily when we are not confused, distracted, or suppressed by beliefs that create fear, anger, and hatred of ourselves, others, and the world around us.

Chapter 3
Natural and Normal
(Skimming the Surface)

03:01 Snow in North Dakota in
June may not be normal,
but it is not unnatural.

03:02 The opposite of natural is
something not of nature.

03:03 Everything of this
universe is of nature.

03:04 Societies develop
norms of standards.

03:05 When actions do not forcefully
impact another there is logic for neutrality.

03:06 From beyond the physical universe
humanity receives it understanding of
unconditional love, truth, wisdom, and bliss.

03:07 The potential of humanity is founded
on an uplifting supernatural reasoning.

03:08 When acting from its earthly natures humankind
is dominating, judgmental, and egocentric.

03:09 When humankind is in its uplifted supernatural self
it knows unconditional love, truth, wisdom, and bliss.

03:10 Happiness is a Divine state;
domination is an earthly state.

03:11 Plants and animals do not display
an uplifting supernatural essence.

03:12 Domestic animals are
bred to behave as they do.

03:13 Plants and animals are elevated but not
made human by training or domestication.

03:14 Unconditional love is founded on a
greater appreciation of circumstances.

03:15 With conditions, people fall out of
love if requirements are not met.

03:16 Unconditional love is
not turned off and on.

03:17 Plants and animals do
not display behaviors of truth.

03:18 Plants and animals are
programmed with no true individuality.

03:19 Plants and animals do not
display behaviors of wisdom.

03:20 Plants and animals are
devoid of intellect.

03:21 Plants and animals are not intensely
cognizant of the events around them.

03:22 Humans will risk death and can begin to
communicate the immensity of that sentiment.

03:23 Humans can postulate concepts and ideals
to express personal beliefs and phenomenon.

03:24 People can gain greater
understanding of what is around them.

03:25 Standards set norms for society;
going beyond the norm is natural.

                    03:26 Logic reflects the thoughtful;
                    emotions often reveal the thoughtless.

03:27 One could seek to live
by nature or norms.

                    03:28 One cannot live life as
                    meaningful and deny greater things.

03:29 The question is begged,
"Why would one not seek self-improvement?"

                    03:30 Self-improvement is found in the
                    balance between logic and emotion.

03:31 In balance we find more:
love, composure, and opportunity.

                    03:32 Out of balance we find more;
                    jealousy, drama, and arrogance.

03:33 Most lives will have a mixture
of logic and emotion.

Chapter 3
Natural and Normal
(Entering the Waters)

- The standards we set for ourselves, or are set for us, do not always reflect every possibility, acceptable or otherwise.

- Because humankind has the potential for reason we realize we are not incidental clumps of earth but harbingers of vast unfulfilled realities.

- The sentiments, profundities, and sheer happiness accessible only by humankind set it above all other life forms.

- We appreciate the need for order yet understand new discoveries are often made beyond its limit.

- To conduct our lives with the greatest of care we seek a balance between logic and emotion, composure and drama, nature and norms.

Chapter 3
Natural and Normal
(Deeper Depths)

Natural: meaning from nature or of nature.
Normal: meaning conforming to a standard.

03:01 Snow falls in North Dakota in December. This is natural. It is even normal. Snow falls in North Dakota in June. While this is not normal, it is not unnatural. For it to be unnatural it would have to come from some other source than nature, which June snow in North Dakota does not. Nature creates snow however you wish to look at it. So what could possibly be an unnatural source of anything, let alone snow?

03:02 An antonym to natural is not abnormal it is unnatural. This begs the question, **"What is unnatural?"** With surface regard, there is no source of anything we encounter in this world that is not of nature. As we look around us all we see is nature. Humankind is a part of nature. The list of objects and forces that do not have origins in nature seems empty.

03:03 Everything of this universe is of nature. So it can be said that aberrant behavior is natural. Due to the fact that it has departed from the accepted standard of behavior it is merely **abnormal**, yet not unnatural.

03:04 Beyond this comparison of the varieties of nature, where all things are natural, and by that notion everything potentially acceptable, there is vexation concerning the origins of particular actions. This is why, but not how, societies develop standards.

03:05 When actions do not forcefully impact another there is logic for neutrality. When one's actions effects the individual alone, the public's emotional response is understandable but does not warrant the creation of law to intercede. Someone's actions may impact them physically and emotionally yet can also influence others to choose actions they otherwise would not. When people do not act on their own behalf, they choose to not, or are truly unable to access that one thing that sets humankind apart from every other thing on this planet. That one thing is a **supernatural** essence, uniquely focused though humankind, as manifested in the concepts and ideals developed and refined by humankind over millennia.

03:06 Humankind has recognized concepts and ideals that touch a core of our existence that parts humanity from every other life form along the lines of **unconditional love**, **truth**, **wisdom**, and **bliss**. Thoughtful individuals have come to accept this uplifting supernatural essence as originating from beyond the boundaries of the body and the simple functions of the brain. The source of this supernatural essence is ascribed to a logic so profound that it is also accountable for a form of Divine self-governance that is called Natural Law.

03:07 Humankind did not create **Natural Law** but can choose to abide by it. The laws of humans more often reflect the finite nature of humans and not the flawless form of nature. Natural Law emphasizes individual worth and moral duty. The perfection of human reasoning is at the foundation for the relevance of Natural Law.

03:08 When acting upon the stage of human pursuits, displaying **earthly natures**, humankind produces natural results. These include; wars of domination, struggle for survival, judgment, building of cities, projection of personalities, egocentric acts, and a base appreciation of art, cuisine, and comforts.

03:09 When humankind rises into their uplifted supernatural nature they bring forth works of, unconditional love, truth, wisdom, and bliss.

03:10 The tonic to the uplifted supernatural nature of humankind is **bliss**. The tonic to the nature of the earthbound human is **domination**. Domination is natural. But it is only the most desirable behavior to a being that is limited to the natures that spring from the physical universe.

03:11   If exalted supernatural behaviors were products of nature than other life forms beyond humans would display these natures. This is not the case. Plants and animals do not display behavior predicated on unconditional love, truth, wisdom, and bliss.

03:12   Owners of pets will tell you that their pet displays **unconditional love**. This is not the case. Domestic animals are bred and trained to behave as they do. Relatively, most domestic pets are simple pieces of software programmed to respond to certain stimuli. On a base level, domestic animals respond to the same fundamental activity of an earthly love that humans seek in their earthly nature.

03:13   Over centuries and millennia humankind has formed a bond that tightly connects humanity with a variety of **domesticated animals**. This bond imbued these species with a significant resonance that drew the breeds closer to humanity. This connection reveals a great deal of our heart along with the genes these animals were drawn from. We cannot disregard what has accumulated in these animals. Because they are not equal to humans, we ought not elevate them to human status. In reverence for life we give to these species what we give to each other in being humane. In our emotions we struggle as we see something of humanity in them.

03:14 Unconditional love is founded on a greater appreciation of circumstances. Humans can love beyond what is perceived as desirable behavior. We open our hearts without condition, to offer support. We love and are neutral toward some to project and protect ourselves. This is our process. People rarely display what is thought to be unconditional love toward all. Yet in moments we can experience **boundless love** for ourselves, others, and the world around us.

03:15 Often if certain requirements are not met people fall out of what they call love. They fall out of this love because it was never truly unconditional love. Simply put the arrangement they had with their partner was acceptable and provided the **desired results** to keep them engaged.

03:16 Once the benefits slow, or stop, what was thought of as love disappears. That is not unconditional, that is appreciation for response and more likely reflects an earthly love. Someone may end a relationship to protect him or herself whether physically, emotionally, or financially and still unconditionally love the past partner. If they come to hate that past partner there was no unconditional love previously, only appreciation and earthly love.

03:17 Plants and animals do not display behaviors of **truth**. There are no plant or animal courts or philosophers. Regardless of the projections of personality onto plants and animals there is no true individuality within a species. Any evidence to the contrary is merely invalid observations that do not satisfy the criterion for individuality. Character and markings may identify an individual object yet these lack creativity and originality essential to individuality which has its basis in truth.

03:18 If a wasp decided on its own to create honeycombs that were triangular, square, pent-angular, octagonal, or any other form then hexagonal, right next to the formations of other wasp of the same species making hexagonal honeycombs, that could be **individuality**. But that does not happen. Because the instincts that direct these animals are base behaviors of nature. Wasp were making these formations a long time ago and continue in the same fashion today.

03:19 Plants and animals do not display behaviors of **wisdom**. The observational powers necessary to create wisdom are not present. There are no innovations produced by these life forms, nor the understanding to master natural phenomenon. Plants and animals show no signs of justice for the innocent. Plants and animals show no signs of conscience that they can convey at anytime in their existence. Here instincts are often mistaken as signs of intense cognition. Everything in the physical universe is **spiritually** connected to the Source of our origin. Yet the cognizant level which humankind has achieved is not evidenced in the plants, animals, and the objects that surround us. If these things knowingly have a greater connection to the Source than humanity, and if we **transgress**, we will be the **recipients**, from them, of the acceptance and forgiveness that we strive to make more completely a pattern in our nature.

03:20   Plants and animals do not display wisdom because plants and animals are devoid of **intellect**. This discussion centers upon the understanding, ordering, and attribution of **sentience**, **cognizance**, and **sapience**.

03:21   These things are not cognizant of the world and vast events surrounding them in ways that would make them experience notions and intuition. The sensing of herd companionship or rivalry is merely instinctive. There is no evidence of any wisdom that transpires or is honed in these life forms. Training is the closest any plant or animal can come to displaying intelligence. Which of course is not intelligence. Without intelligence there is no **bliss**, merely the relaxation of the **fight-or-flight** response.

03:22   Humans on the other hand display forms of unconditional love. The sacrifices of life and limb, with forethought as to the consequences, show a commitment with some unconditional elements. Humans can verbally explain this thought process and will admit when they rise to a level that is beyond their ability to communicate in words. This is not a failing on the part of communication but more likely an acknowledgement of the immensity of the sentiment.

03:23   Humans can **forgive** without forgetting. Humans can postulate concepts and ideals to express personal beliefs, and phenomenon. They also can express the complexities of justice, liberty, honor, and logic.

03:24 With their experiences, people can learn not only to make better decisions but also to have greater understanding of those around them. At the epitome of human life an overview of this existence can be obtained by humankind through reflecting upon life, our place within it, and things greater than the self.

03:25 The standards of life are set to create parameters for normal social living yet **going beyond the norm is the norm** for the expansion of humankind. The individual is always the focal point for the expansion of humankind. Reaching beyond our limitations has become the hallmark of humankind. The expansion of behavior goes in both productive and counterproductive directions. This is mirrored by the thoughtful and thoughtless natures of humanity.

03:26 Logic is reflected in the thoughtful, while emotion often reveals the thoughtless. If not intrusive, thoughtless behavior can add to society without the need to be consciously considered. More often thoughtless behavior is less-loving actions taken to create a sense of security in the actor. This is easily within the emotional capacity of humans. **Logically** it makes less sense. To the emotionalist it is acceptable and desirable.

03:27 One could seek to live by nature or norms. For many it is normal to **struggle**. Instead of referring to their experience as a struggle, those who have enough of an understanding of greater things clearly view their experience as occasionally facing challenges. The former is emotion charged, while the latter is logical. Logic points humankind in the direction of the uplifting supernatural essence. Our **evolution** toward the exalted supernatural state of Divinity is a vast movement away from a lack of self-awareness as we develop a conscious communion with the **Source** of our Creation. This expansion of self is inevitable.

03:28   One cannot live a life they deem as meaningful and deny greater things. Anyone who permanently struggles must deny greater things, or admit to the charade of using greater things as a mask. One cannot believe in greater things and then live a life as if those greater things do not exist. As contradictory as this may seem it is also natural, due to the nature of the earthly human and the unfounded need and selfish desire to manipulate events into what they believe is their favor.

03:29   Where all this comes together is in the following questions and the actions that result from asking:

- **Why would one wish to not improve their life?**

- **If one knew the mechanics to improve their life would they pursue improvement?**

- **How can one know the path to betterment and not engage the actions to improve their condition?**

03:30   The answer to these questions and the answer to these conditions are in developing, in one's life, a more productive balance between **logic** and **emotion**.

03:31   If one assures themselves they have balance in their life then logically certain realities will be present and other conditions will be limited. Present will be; love, self-confidence, composure, opportunity, creativity, patience, acceptance, and other attributes.

03:32   Many emotions are desirable for what they add to life. When emotions become less-desirable limiting these emotions can help to balance one's perspective. In a balanced life there will be limited: melodrama, fretful competition, resistance, arrogance, chaos, frustration, judgment, and many more dysfunctional behaviors.

03:33 Most lives will have logical and emotional, attributes and behaviors. How this effects the individual will be determined by the attributes and behaviors the person feels and displays. Depressing emotions can be challenging. There are strategies for diminishing emotional depression that are properly applied with the support of the appropriate assistance. The prime option is to engage the possibilities and never give up seeking balance.

The Sinker seeks to usurp liberty and life and speaks in words designed to **manipulate**, **placate**, and **mislead**. Often they use calls of, "sacrifice," to obfuscate their goal.

A sacrifice is an offering given from the heart and without coercion. It is sacred and holy. By using the word, "**sacrifice,**" the Sinker bludgeons others to submit to their will. **"Do this for the children,"** is another favorite phrase constructed to allow no quarter for disapproval of the Sinker's plan.

Their desire is to bend others to their destructive will and to control without regard for the individual. Those who do not allow others to engage **Natural Law** and do as they see fit exhibit the Sinker mentality. This pattern inexorably leads to the utter destruction of lives.

Chapter 4
Uplifting and Suppressing
(Skimming the Surface)

04:01 Between management and labor,
one cannot be more valuable than the other.

04:02 With an endless supply of jobs
and workers both lose value.

04:03 Supply and demand affects everything.

04:04 In negotiations there comes
a time for a decision.

04:05 Leverage is lost when one enters
a negotiation with a need to strike a deal.

04:06 When emotions dominate business
negotiations, the process suffers.

04:07 When one is truly free in negotiations
a more beneficial outcome is possible.

04:08 For the chooser, the more choices the better.

04:09 If two parties are at odds one will
be more logical and the other more emotional.

04:10 In confrontation, one side will have more positive
solutions and the other will feel more without control.

04:11 Once emotional frustration
comes to a head action will follow.

04:12 Emotions that seek to change agreements
reveal a lack of freedom in negotiations.

04:13 Logic will seek to break any
impasse only when the benefit is found.

04:14 Emotionalism will either collapse
in defeat or strike out in rage.

04:15 Violence is predicated on
an emotional position.

04:16 What derails free negotiations is manifold.

04:17 Coercion can stifle one's right of conscience.

04:18 Openly having a belief is everyone's right.

04:19 Negotiations deemed vital
will impair free negotiations.

04:20 Proper perspective can
produce benefits for all involved.

04:21 Market forces determine what
is produced and what skills are needed.

04:22 In negotiations, one party
will have the upper hand.

04:23 Making guarantees is a tenuous business practice.

04:24 Skills become less valuable when
they become widely available.

04:25 An entrepreneur produces;
a craftsman produces.

04:26 People who do not develop
themselves diminish their value.

04:27 Sustainable results are not products
solely of desperation, or anger.

04:28 On a daily basis a person
negotiates for many different things.

04:29 Negotiate means, "not leisure" -
leisure means, "be allowed."

04:30 In all we do we either negotiate or allow.

04:31 "Life must be lived as play." - Plato

Chapter 4
Uplifting and Suppressing
(Entering the Waters)

- Whether as an employer or an employee every person is their own boss, working, in a free society, at the job they accept.

- If someone dislikes the circumstances of their business/employment they very likely have the ability to change their circumstance.

- A reasonable person will first seek change in a situation they would like to see changed. While an emotional person will respond with lament or rage toward a circumstance they dislike.

- Negotiations are how we make our way in life. Moving around, exchanging value for value, or working out the terms for an agreement, negotiations are almost everywhere.

- Leisure is the only thing that exists outside of negotiations.

- We either seek to arrange circumstances to our liking or we allow life to be as it is and then decide how we wish to partake of it.

Chapter 4

Uplifting and Suppressing
(Deeper Depths)

04:01 There has been an ongoing debate between the factions of management and workers for a while now. **Management** says, "Without our investment of wealth and our expertise in the market place, workers would not have a job." **Workers** say, "Without the sweat of laborers, factories would be idle." Is one more right than the other?

04:02 Management can higher other workers, workers can take employment at other factories. This makes sense as long as there are enough workers and enough factories. But if a worker has limited skills they are limited as to where they can seek employment. If the labor force is limited or collective in their position, management might find it harder to hire workers. It is easier today than in the past, yet moving a factory has several costs that can inhibit such an occurrence.

04:03 This brings into focus the law of **supply** and **demand**. The supplies in these two cases are factory positions and the workers to fill the positions. The demand in these two cases is the same, the factory demand for workers and the worker's demand for gainful employment. How these two do not arrive at a mutually beneficial agreement is found in the values each ascribes to the other and themselves.

04:04 In **negotiations** there comes a time when a person must decide, up or down, if they will take a particular offer. If handled in an honorable and logical manner this is done dispassionately with a simple "yes thank you," or respectful, "no thank you." There will be an appropriate time later to revel in success or develop another approach to the desired end.

04:05 When one enters a negotiation with a need to strike a deal one has weakened their bargaining posture. If the deal must be made because one feels an acute need for employment or one must not allow a factory to sit idle the negotiator is dealing from a lessened position.

04:06   When emotions dominate business negotiations, the process suffers.

04:07   Entering a negotiation with an, **"I have to have this!"** mentality does not bode well for a profitable outcome. So if the parties are thinking, "If I don't get this job I'm sunk!" or "If I can't put workers to a task I am going to lose money!" dealings will be pressurized and skewed. When one is truly free in negotiations a more beneficial outcome is more likely.

04:08   If a factory owner has a lot of labor to choose from the best fit can be found at a lower cost. If the worker has valuable skills, and more than one set of skills, they will have more choices and more value. If management has a small or restricted labor pool to choose from and does not feel free to respectfully say "no thank you" and to idle their production they will feel forced to make a deal they will not feel fully benefits them. If a worker has a limited skill set and few employment prospects they will feel the pinch to make a deal before someone else takes an available job opportunity.

04:09   If one, or both sides, gets into a situation where they feel they would have liked to have had a different outcome the emotions of the predicament, if not completely crushing the person's spirit, will continue to build until there is a venting of frustration. Because these two sides are at odds one side will be predicated more on logic and the other more on emotion.

04:10   **One side** will have more positive solutions and the other will feel more without control. If both parties are predicated more on logic there will be a suitable and stable agreement and if both are predicated more on emotion there will not be a sustainable agreement, or an agreement at all.

04:11 Once the emotional frustration comes to a head action will follow. The forms this action could take are numerous. On the part of management there may be a lock out. On the part of the workers there may be a walk out. Both implement what should have come in the negotiation stage by either party respectfully saying, "no thank you."

04:12 By whoever acts in this manner it will be revealed that they were, for whatever reason, unable to honestly and freely negotiate. Nothing has changed since the contracts were approved. Changes in the parties can be attributed to desires not addressed at the negotiation table. If all concerns were not addressed the contract should not have been approved. Some will hide their intentions, accepting an agreement to only later seek adjustment to the agreement when the other side has become more dependent on having the agreement. What can keep an honest party from freely negotiating will be explored later in this chapter.

04:13 When an impasse arises a logical response could be, "this is an impasse that I am choosing to not entertain because it does not benefit me suitably." At this same juncture the emotional response will be one of lament over lost wages or lost earnings. Logic will seek to break any impasse only when the benefit is found. If the emotional side does not see the logic in an offer the impasse grows leading from the inactive stage of lament to the active emotional stage of aggressive behavior.

04:14 **Emotionalism** will either collapse in defeat or strike out in rage. A situation may start with a lock out or a walk out and without a remedy move to other acts of coercion to gain the desired end.

04:15 Whether intimidation of physical harm or damage and loss of property, both are predicated from the weakened position of emotion. Only if the other party succumbs to these emotions will this ploy produce an outcome that will halt the undesirable situation. But through this method no fully satisfying agreement can be forged. The resulting situation will sooner or later lead to another emotionally frustrating impasse. The reason for this is the lack of perspective on the values of the parties in the negotiation.

04:16 Honesty in business dealings is a measure of integrity. Though people, corporations, and unions who are dishonest care little for their integrity. What keeps one, or both parties, from freely negotiating is manifold. Whether as a unit, or as an individual, if the **right of conscience** is not intact some form of coercion has come to bear, limiting the rights and freedom of the effected negotiator.

04:17 The right of conscience is the desire, and the airing of that desire, to undertake what is thought, for whatever reason, to be the appropriate action. This should withstand open scrutiny in the clear light of day. This also requires an atmosphere free of **coercion** from an outside group such as: co-owners, co-workers, the media, the government, or the public.

04:18 Openly holding a belief as to an appropriate course of action is everyone's right. Feeling as though an agreement must be reached at any cost will inhibit free negotiations. If a deal cannot be walked away from the freedom to negotiate has been severely hampered. An offer that cannot be refused violates an individual's **freedom**.

04:19 If one is dealing from a state-of-mind that views the negotiations as vitally important, and an absolute necessity, free negotiations are impaired. For whatever reason these views are held, the negotiator's position is weakened.

04:20 Perspective on a situation is important if there is to be benefits for all involved. Without workers a factory sits idle. Without a factory, workers sit idle. Necessities being what they are workers with drive will not sit idle for long. A self-motivated person will find some way to express their purpose, making ends meet. To what extent this individual will go will show their capacity for **survival**. A factory is simply a building containing work areas and tools. How those aspects are engaged is up to the ingenuity of the factory owner(s).

04:21 Market forces play a role in determining what a successful factory produces and what skills are needed from the labor force. The **flexibility** of management and labor bode well for satisfying and sustainable partnerships. For either side to offer a win-win agreement, a benefit needs to be provided. The party that is first acting, the offering of jobs or the offering of labor, will first recognize benefits. Then for an offer to make sense the benefits need to be recognized by those receiving the offer. Then finally the parties will receive the greatest potential from the agreement by respecting and appreciating these benefits. Without this balance an agreement will unravel leading to emotional frustration and future impasse.

04:22 Here is a potential scenario - **Management** offers labor a limited number of positions with wages set at the current accepted rates. Management makes this offer to maximize profits. Labor wants guarantees of wages, benefits, and retirement packages with incremental increases over time regardless of sales. For management to provide this they must start with lower wages or higher productivity levels, or both. To do otherwise would not be profitable in the long run. One party has the upper hand.

04:23 Here is another potential scenario - The pool of skilled and trainable workers is plentiful. **Collectively**, they seek the most profitable arrangements for themselves. The factory owner needs workers and receives an offer from labor to fill that need. Labor wants assurances of job security and benefits. The factory owner has a general confidence that the product made will have a strong marketability though competition does exist. To guarantee security and benefits with limited foreknowledge of future sales is a tenuous business practice. One party has the upper hand.

04:24 To provide for and to protect the rights of the individual, workers organize into a single front. Whether this is done from a position of strength or weakness is a matter of perspective. Yet one is more correct that the other. The banding together of craft skills dates back thousands of years. Sharing these skills outside the designated circles could result in severe **repercussions**. If the skills became highly available the value of the work achieved through the skill would be diminished. With widely available skills, management would find it easier and less expensive to obtain a work force. This all comes back to an overlooked constant.

04:25 An **entrepreneur** sets out with financial backing and business knowledge and the purpose of producing something. The question is what. A **craftsman** sets out with desire, skill, and knowledge to make something with their hands. The question is what. If either accepts an answer to their question that does not satisfy their purpose on a **soul-type** level they are agreeing to the investing of themselves into something that at some point will potentially ring hollow in their life experience.

04:26 These individuals have not come to understand and value themselves enough to pursue the development of their **circumstance** as to uncover and fulfill their life purpose. To some degree, when they discover this shortcoming, they will either collapse in defeat or strike out in rage. For an emotional person if neither of those things happens they have not sufficiently discovered their disregard for their purpose. Pursuing one's purpose is as valuable as fulfilling it. Finding satisfaction, of an acceptable degree, is not beyond the possibilities of a diverted life. With acceptance fulfillment can be found in many endeavors. Yet of the questioning crafted by the judgmental mind regrets bite deeply.

04:27 Though potentially a pivotal moment, silent desperation, or full-blown anger, in and of itself, will not produce sustainable results. But as a **catalyst** combined with thoughtful reflection, optimism, and acceptance, prospects will be revealed.

04:28 On a daily basis we as individuals negotiate for a wide variety of positions and assistance in our **endeavors**. When we reach an agreement with others, we have been a **negotiator**. When we make our way around an obstacle, be it mental or physical, we have been a **negotiator**. When we convert cash or checks for products or services we **negotiate**. We do this all in the course of business, including the business of living life.

04:29 The word negotiate comes from the Latin **"negotium"** which breaks down as neg - "not" and otium - "leisure." So when we are not taking care of business we are at leisure which comes from another Latin word **"licere"** meaning "be allowed." With that we can see life as one of two modes, business or leisure.

04:30 How we approach, act, and follow through in any situation will reveal whether we are in business or leisure mode - if we seek our desire through negotiation or if we allow what will happen, to happen. Both have a role in our experience yet any situation will call more for one than the other. Discerning which, is the question at hand. How we look at the time we have and how we engage that time produces different results.

04:31 **William Faulkner** is credited with having said, "Clocks slay time . . . time is dead as long as it is being clicked off by little wheels; only when the clock stops does time come to life." And long before William Faulkner it is reported that **Plato** said, "Life must be lived as play." Both quotes emphasize the value and importance of leisure.

Chapter 5
Wealth and Time
(Skimming the Surface)

05:01 Only a person with material wealth
ought to decide what will happen to it.

05:02 A gift is something given without
expecting anything in return.

05:03 Someone who views life as lacking
is easily seen as mostly emotional.

05:04 Investments include time and effort.

05:05 A legitimate financial empire is the
property of the one who produces it.

05:06 What someone produces represents his or
her creativity, awareness, and fortitude of action.

05:07 An entrepreneur will focus over
a lifetime and likely amass wealth.

05:08 Government will intercede to tax wealth.

05:09 To justify taking more, the government
plays to the emotions of people.

05:10 All investments can be a
steppingstone to greater things.

05:11 A thoughtful employer will do all they can to
provide mutually beneficial opportunities to employees.

05:12 An entrepreneur's life and
business are greatly intertwined.

05:13 A worker amasses wealth
in the form of knowledge.

05:14 Money alone does not clothe,
nor feed, nor shelter.

05:15 Ingenuity and fabrication
are invaluable resources.

05:16 An inventor's wealth is their brainpower.

05:17 Workers, laborers, and craftsmen invest
time to accumulate skills and knowledge.

05:18 Without resources and people,
greater things are not accomplished.

05:19 Greater goals will forever loom beyond our grasp.

05:20 If one does not strive to accumulate
wealth it is likely none will come.

Chapter 5
Wealth and Time
(Entering the Waters)

- A societal structure that claims the fruit of the citizenry's industry as its own for illegitimate activities is unjust.

- Taxing the least possible and leaving the bulk of earnings with the producer is the most productive and fairest to all.

- What a lawful person produces represents his or her creativity, awareness, and fortitude of action.

- Governments do not create wealth and must intercede in wealth formation to claim a portion of that wealth to provide for the common good.

- Governments are populated by people and people are subject to human nature which can easily devolve into meddlesome and misguided efforts to influence.

- Both the entrepreneur and the craftsman, if aware and focused, are working toward greater goals then their current situation.

- We are the lives we live and the hopes we hold dear. If one does not work, nothing is completed.

Chapter 5
Wealth and Time
(Deeper Depths)

05:01 Financial wealth can be stolen (by or from someone), created, and also given or inherited. It can only be inherited if the person with the money chooses to whom the money will be given. That may seem obvious. Normally, it is not given to someone if that person does not know the benefactor to whom the wealth belongs. Only a person, who has wealth, can rightly decide to bequeath or give their money away.

05:02 A **gift** is something that is simply given - without expectation of something in return. This is true of any gift. In the real world there is nothing unfair about inheriting wealth. If someone were to give another person a gift and then, out of the woodworks, a voice announces that the gift is not really the possession of the receiver, but actually public property, there would be friction. A bicycle is given to a child - "No," the voice says, "The bicycle belongs to the public." This scenario seems to lack logic, though it contains a great deal of **emotion**.

05:03 Someone who views life as lacking, or unfair, can easily be understood to be more emotional than logical. Without exception, lack can be found in every life. There is the timeless gift giving inquiry, "What do you give the man who has everything?" You can be assured there **IS** something. Even if it is as simple, yet vital, as love. Possessions and wealth can accumulate in many ways and forms.

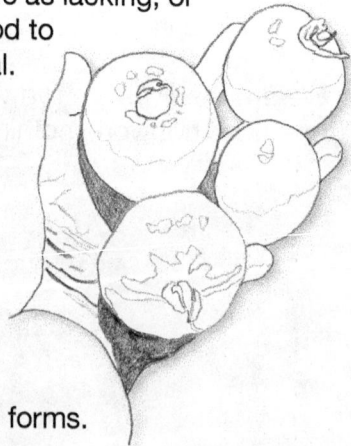

05:04 Here is a potential scenario - a person could buy tomatoes for one cent and at their stand, sell them for two cents. After investing 12 cents in tomatoes and spending (read; investing), two hours selling the tomatoes on a street corner this **entrepreneur** now has 24 cents. Regardless of the numbers, the burgeoning wealth generated by the day of selling tomatoes does in fact belong to the individual who invested their money and time, hardly to mention their effort, to generate the 24 cents in wealth. They started with one penny. They bought and sold, always reinvesting their principle and profit back into more tomatoes.

05:05 The original penny could have come as pay for services rendered, given as a gift, or even loaned to the entrepreneur. However, by the time the effort has accumulated to the point 24 cents has been earned it does in fact belong to the one who generated it.

05:06 There are those who would say it is only 24 cents. It is only 24 cents because they cannot get emotionally charged up over such a small amount. Try taking the 24 cents away from the person who risked their 12 cents and spent two hours standing on the street corner selling tomatoes. The money is a whole lot more than 24 cents. The money represents that person's creativity, awareness, and **fortitude of action**.

05:07 Those two hours were a part, albeit a small part, of the person's life. Regardless of how small the segment, those two hours could have been spent differently and those two hours cannot be lived again. How it was spent returned the investment along with the profit. It is quite likely this entrepreneur will reinvest the 24 cents to generate more profit and through this habit, over a lifetime, likely amass great wealth.

05:08 At some point, under the auspices of doing public good, the government will intercede to tax the wealth generated. The public generally accepts this concept. The appropriateness of how much the government demands is another discussion based on what the government plans to do with the **tax money**.

05:09 To justify taking more money some in government will play to the emotions of those whose financial wealth is not as abundant. The reason for taking more is to gain the support of those who will be receiving the value of the tax dollars and of those who are emotionally overwrought by the concept of someone having abundant wealth.

05:10 The factory owner(s) invest their wealth and their time to make something for themselves. The owner of the tomato selling concern was fortunate to require only one employee and that they were available to take the position. But a small operation, such as a tomato stand, is a steppingstone to greater things. Over the length of this person's life they will likely not continue selling tomatoes for a **penny profit**.

05:11 If they stay with selling produce they will likely work to amass greater wealth with which to invest in a more profitable business. This could be a bigger stand, a cart, or a storefront. At some point this lone businessperson will probably need to employ help. When this happens if the business owner has appropriate appreciation for the value of the **employee** they will do all that they reasonably can to provide a mutually beneficial arrangement to that employee.

05:12 More often than not the factory/business owner has put a great deal into their enterprise and in all likelihood the business is **inextricably intertwined** with their life and the pursuit of their life experience. They consider their life and their business on equivalant planes.

05:13 Formost, a worker amasses wealth in the form of **knowledge**. The expertise gained through the instruction and apprenticeship a laborer engages in will accumulate throughout their life and compound greatly. Without this knowledge their production of goods and services cease.

05:14 **Money** alone does not clothe, nor feed, nor shelter. Raw materials do not educate, or transport, or heal. For the betterment of all involved, resources, (money/effort), begets resources, (raw materials), beget resources, (tools), for the improvement of lives and experiences. But for the resources of raw material to be converted into the resources of tools, other resources must enter the equation.

05:15 Those resources are **ingenuity** and **fabrication**. A pile of iron ore is not a hammer until ingenuity and fabrication are employed. The procedures of smelting and forging may be centuries old but, at some point, these procedures were ingeniously invented and refined by someone. Long after the methods of turning ore into a workable metal someone came up with a tool design that was later used to produce a tool, which was later used to bring about some other desire. Whether it is building a house, probing the earth for resources, or researching for medical discoveries the end user could not provide their talent without the talents that provided the tools that aided them along the way.

05:16 An **inventor** makes a device to generate electricity. Without the workers who then produced the hundreds and thousands of electric generators the public would be waiting a long time for the inventor to fill the demand. And while the inventor was filling that demand other inventions in that person's mind would not be brought forward. As well, the skills in fabricating machinery possessed by the workers would lay untapped.

05:17 The worker, laborer, and craftsman all invest their life into the **accumulation** of skills and knowledge, which they can then bring to bear in the production of goods and services.

05:18 While the involvement of people is essential, the raw materials needed also have great value. For without either, nothing is accomplished. Without the investment of wealth, however one describes it (capital, skills and talents, work sites, genius, etc.), nothing is done, nothing is gained, and greater goals are **inapproachable**.

05:19 As one strives to achieve, greater goals will forever loom beyond our grasp - this is human history. Somehow we continue to work on the possible while only being able to glimpse the fantastical that will likely be reached by later generations. This is why we work. If we focus on what we do not have we will only see what we cannot achieve.

05:20 A person goes through life working to accumulate wealth in its many forms, or they do not. If one chooses to not strive to amass wealth they will most likely not possess wealth. The ability to embark upon wealth accumulation is different for everyone. A laborer may not become a wealthy financial person. A person of financial wealth may not become a valued craftsman. Each has their role and yet each is free to embark upon any course of action they desire - a doctor that becomes a farmer, or a farmer that becomes a doctor. Who they serve first, and why, will determine their **success** and the accumulation of what they call wealth.

Chapter 6
Forms Of Wealth
(Skimming the Surface)

06:01 Everyone lives, having been
given a singularly unique life.

06:02 Some people strive to control elements
of life that are beyond their control.

06:03 Appreciating the treasures of
this life is done through openness.

06:04 Time is a form of wealth.

06:05 More time always appears after time passes.

06:06 One cannot assert leverage
in negotiations with time.

06:07 Arrangements that are not mutually
beneficial unravel or are somehow unfulfilling.

06:08 Acceptance, but not capitulation, is the
counter-balance to attempted manipulation.

06:09 Making allowances for the unknown to appear
is risky yet potentially productive.

06:10 Nothing is gained if the wealth
of life and time are not employed.

06:11 Life and time produces an uplifting
experience if acceptance is willfully given.

06:12 Over time, listening to one's heart
will reveal, to them, who and what they are.

06:13 Life is the ultimate gift
and the ultimate form of wealth.

06:14 Our contributions are in all ways
beyond the two dimensional world.

Chapter 6
Forms of Wealth
(Entering the Waters)

- Life and time are the greatest gifts ever given.

- So much of life is outside of our control.

- Our best hope is to influence and inspire.

- Time is of great value.

- Combining life and time, one can achieve great things.

- What we do has the potential to create influence and inspiration far beyond the life and moment in which we act.

Chapter 6
Forms Of Wealth
(Deeper Depths)

06:01 One thing everyone on this planet has is life, each inhabiting a singularly unique life. This is not something we had to negotiate. It was given to us as the **greatest gift possible**. Not every life is without particularities that could be thought of as drawbacks or shortcomings. But nearly every instance can be overcome to a satisfactory degree as to allow the greater aspects of life to be engaged providing fulfillment.

06:02 There are people who can enumerate situations, relationships, or events that they would have negotiated differently. They are seeing these circumstances as business or competition and certainly not leisure. They approach these circumstances as negotiations that must be dealt with. They do not approach these circumstances with leisure allowing them to be who or what they are. Instead they take a position that a circumstance must be transformed to their desire. To them this **transformation** is quite often vitally important, and an absolute necessity. If this were not the case they would allow the circumstance to unfold and be what it is.

06:03 Life is a **treasure** and in so a form of wealth. The plethora of possibilities that are available to those who are open to them are a bountiful wealth. There are those who will dispute this perspective. Appreciating the treasures of this life is done through openness. Seeing positive in any situation takes the leisurely eye for allowing every situation, relationship, and event to play out without discarding the interaction before it has been allowed to yield its potential - then to receive the product of the interaction for what it is.

06:04 To allow situations, relationships, and events to play out we invest another form of wealth that has been given to us . . . **time**. The idea that time is fleeting is the misplaced emphasis of a negotiation. The necessity to conform time to our needs is a **never successful** business arrangement.

06:05   Time may be made to fit into a frame at one point but before one realizes, time slips pass never to be regained. In that occurrence is seen one of the amazing attributes of time. More time always shows up right after time elapses. Our time in this life may be limited but that is more a function of us and not of time.

06:06   As our experience changes and goes through time those approaching life as a negotiation begin to feel the loss of the strength of their position. Sticking to their business approach their internal discussion turns toward assertively or aggressively bringing leverage to obtain success over the obstacles they encounter in their life.

06:07   Any arrangement that has been struck, that is not mutually beneficial to all parties, will eventually unravel or somehow be **unfulfilling**. With this, the possibility of blame and recrimination will likely surface, exacerbating the situation, fueling further disintegration.

06:08   When feeling the loss of control over things outside our control, acceptance can be an appropriate counter-balance to these feelings. With proper boundaries, we can create space and accept non-threatening situations, relationships, and events for what they are. The methods of business are active, controlling, and calculated. The best approach to business, whether in life or commerce, provides unfilled areas to make allowance for the undetermined to propagate. Through this, acceptance is cultivated in an unmanaged way. In this manner risk enters the equation.

06:09   The potential for productivity found in risk is largely undeterminable. **Risk** must be managed but is recognized as not completely manageable otherwise it would not be considered as risky. Making allowances within a structure for the unknown to appear is risky yet potentially productive. How risky, is the question.

06:10 There will be nothing gained if the wealth of life and time any person possesses is not employed in some endeavor to express and fulfill an uplifting purpose. How much of one's life and time will be devoted to negotiating desired goals will reveal the inner workings of the individual's mind. In their aim to attain prizes and perceived advantages they show how they value life, time, and themselves.

06:11 These greatest of possessions will produce a unique essence in tune with the individual's purpose if **acceptance** is willfully given. This action will facilitate the unfoldment of the participant's life in an upward movement.

06:12 What makes someone an authority or gives weight to their pronouncements can be **spotty**. Yet if someone has listened to their heart for a considerable length of time they will understand who and what they are and will be best positioned to express that which they feel is their true essence. This is a path to fulfilling one's life purpose.

06:13 Life and time are the ultimate gifts and the ultimate forms of **wealth**. Regardless of one's physical condition, proclivities, or abilities, we each have potential for expression and contributing to this world. These contributions do not need to be the material for banner headlines or best selling novels.

06:14 Our contributions are in all ways beyond the two dimensional world. When we contribute we inspire those near us to contribute. As we show those around us what uplifting and loving behavior produces we raise our surroundings. In those actions we swim through life realizing and valuing the Source of the greatest wealth we could ever **hope** to attain.

Thinkers and Sinkers

Chapter 7
Individualism and Communalism
(Skimming the Surface)

07:01 Infants are born without the
greater abilities needed for survival.

07:02 Small children act by
instinct and intuition.

07:03 Young children learn the
means for manipulation.

07:04 Achievement and expression
are human nature.

07:05 Humanity is here today
because of early communities.

07:06 The positive nature of humanity
is found in creating uplifting experiences.

07:07 A variety in roles brought
about the growth of societies.

07:08 In ancient times child
bearing was critical for group survival.

07:09 Societal boundaries can be
stretched when needs are met.

07:10 Schools can educate
and/or indoctrinate.

07:11 The best education teaches
to the students' intellect.

07:12 A person's inner-self can be revealed
if they allow and accept themselves.

07:13 Community does not strictly refer
to the neighborhood one lives in.

07:14 Community is more a
feeling of connection.

07:15 The closes communities are
those joined from the heart.

07:16 Humankind is endlessly creative.

07:17 The human mind brings forward
a continuous flow of cause and effect.

07:18 A role that is not heartfelt
will not be fulfilling.

07:19 A thoughtful person can best
decide their greatest role in society.

07:20 The highest benefit comes when the thoughtful
individual determines their own role.

07:21 The early communal setting helped
shape humanity into what it is today.

07:22 Our communal past was
essential for our survival.

07:23 Our communal past is being
slowly replaced by individualism.

07:24 Communalism will likely
return in the distant future.

07:25 Individualism is here
and integral to present times.

07:26 To abandon individualism
is unconscionable.

07:27 The risk-to-reward
factor is a part of life.

07:28 Life is not directed as,
"evolution by committee."

07:29 Individuals are the driving force
behind the expansion of humanity.

07:30 Being frightened by the
unknown is a part of human nature.

07:31 Being prepared to rise to
challenges is a part of human nature.

07:32 The importance of a moral
code is far reaching.

07:33 Civil laws prohibit behaviors
and strike down infringement of persons.

07:34 Pick one: certain yet limited rewards
or uncertain yet unlimited rewards.

07:35 The thoughtful care for all;
the thoughtless care only for themselves.

Chapter 7
Individualism and Communalism
(Entering the Waters)

- We do not begin life as blank slates. As we grow, our efforts and attention are channeled in a direction. This direction is either of our choosing or as a result of our not choosing.

- Long since past is the age that could properly demand a person living a life for the goals of others.

- Humankind is endlessly creative. When we release the loving expression that is in our heart we reveal our purpose.

- In living a civil life, when one person seeks to dictate to another the first shows their inability to accept what they are not meant to control.

- We stay with what is certain and reap small rewards or risk upon the uncertain with hopes of unlimited rewards.

Chapter 7
Individualism and Communalism
(Deeper Depths)

Child Development

07:01 The development of a newborn begins from a point with almost no bodily control and **no intellectual mastery**.

07:02 Small children innately want to do for themselves, seeking to explore and experiment. Most express confidence in subjects of which they have little understanding. Their world is centered on them. With little concept of others, their thoughts are all they have. They are egocentric. These children **intuitively act** when they have want. With signs of Pavlovian Response they grow to recognize those who will satisfy their wants, yet with no concept of why someone would, or would not, provide for them.

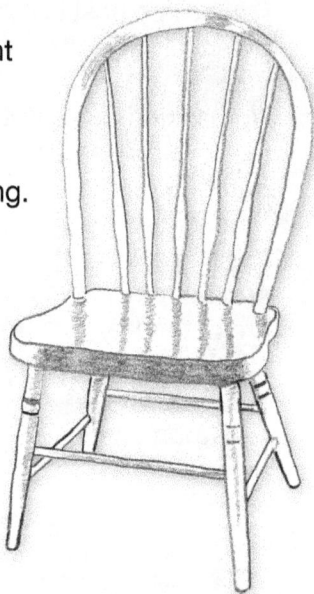

07:03 In their second year of life a child is quickly learning the manipulation they can bring to bear in vocalizing their wants. Although vocalizing is used from the time of birth the two year old is cognitively putting the pieces together. Beginning to assert authority they do not have, they admonish, **"No!"** to the object of their displeasure. This may be mimicking the treatment they have received but they somehow understand the powerful intent of the word.

07:04 Soon to follow will be the declaration, **"Mine!"** Humans have an inborn desire to express themselves, to achieve, and to rise. This is human nature. Within a well-structured life a child will enter into a process of learning to gain the tools for discernment and expression of self. The child is heading for the world of **Thinkers and Sinkers.**

First Came Communalism

07:05 As early humanity struggled for survival, challenges were so great the only path to the future was through the cooperation of community. Whether it was clan, village, or nation the bonds that held the group together were there to assure the continuation of the **bloodline.** A family cannot build upon their experience if there is no progeny.

07:06 The nature of humans to seek and provide an uplifting experience for themselves, their family, and their community echoes our deepest purpose for being. We have evolved to this point by striking out as groups, and later individuals, while representing the positive nature in humankind. This is what **Thinkers** do.

Individualism Found A Place

07:07 It was not until **individuals** in a group could specialize that the expansion of our experience became possible. The movement away from communal and monolithic mindset is a gradual process. Early on, the need for every male to be a hunter was replaced by the development of **technology.** Whether it was stone tools or techniques, fewer hunters were required to fulfill the need of the group.

07:08 Child baring and raising was still of such high importance the **freedom** to express individuality for most females was limited. As slow as it was, change was on the way. Times did change and slowly females rose to prominent positions of leadership. From there they could begin to more greatly express their individuality and creativity.

07:09 When individuality sprouted in the heart only the most forceful of circumstances could keep that expression from being brought forward. As long as the needs of the whole were being met the boundaries could be stretched.

Herd Mentality

07:10 An **education** and the **socializing** offered in an ordinary school setting today are two entirely different things. A rounded education that includes communication skills, mathematics, science, literature, history, critical thinking, and spirituality are only the beginning. Without knowing who and what an individual is in their heart advanced curriculum cannot be prescribed.

07:11 Discovering the unique nature of every student is paramount. Without instructing to the individual all that can be hoped for is to turn out a duplicate of a previous student. Students are individuals. Turning out duplicates only populates the herd. Herds are best managed through strict **conformity** and **communal processes**. To this end all **true individuality** is scorned by the governing ethos.

07:12 Herd mentality is the path of least resistance. This path returns commensurate fruit. Even from the viewpoint of the herd, individuality is held aloft, but their process of true individuality is still evolving. Herd members imitate true individuals. They are learning, in some ways, how it feels to be unique. But without expressing their heart they will never be their unique self. They will only think of themselves as individuals yet never feel comfortable with their inner-self. It is a process. If they **accept** others and **allow** their curiosity to float freely they will discover their path to rise.

Contributions Of The Individual
Out Weight Conformity

07:13 In the modern age, **community** has not lost its meaning but has become redefined with expanded value. Value that reaches out with open arms to embrace the individual and what they have to offer.

07:14 Communities now exist between people who have never physically met. The understanding that we are in this life together forms communities on a multitude of levels. Beliefs, interests, and forms of expression bring people together from across the globe.

07:15 How these individuals become and stay involved in these communities is of their own **free will**. These communities represent an identified essence these people have discovered within themselves. The contributions brought about by the individual are only possible when they shed the influence of the necessity another feels for them to conform.

Nature Fills The Gap

07:16 The **creativity** of humanity endlessly fills the gaps found in the fabric of society. This is not always done seamlessly and without periods of absence but evenly and naturally. Human creativity makes discoveries even before needs are identified. New discoveries come on the tail of previous discoveries. New uses are found for old discoveries and human **curiosity** never stops searching.

07:17 All effects have an originating cause and the human component is another part of nature contributing actions that cause effects. For the Thinker, these effects endlessly bring light to the possibilities for **innovation**.

Contrived Communal Societies

07:18 At any particular time an individual, authority, or structure reflects an **influential mindset**. This can be an uplifting mindset in line with the Thinker mentality or a suppressive mindset found in the Sinker mentality. The presentation of this mindset can vary with time and circumstance. Also, the observer brings a bias to the interpretation of the mindset. Today the fount of human curiosity, creativity, and expression is potentially obstructed when an individual is arbitrarily prescribed a communal role.

07:19 The Thinker can easily, if not uncomfortably, recognize when they are being steered into a communal role that is not in line with their heart. **The Sinker mentality** is revealed if the prescribed role is not aligned with an uplifting mindset. This mindset will foist the want for communal behavior upon individuals who would better serve humanity in an unfettered role inspiring others to uplifting behaviors and existence.

07:20 Determining that an individual is best suited to a **communal experience** ought to be the choice of the individual. When an authority, often self-established, intent on shaping a community, ethnicity, or nation, makes this determination they are possibly discarding the potential of the individual. This curtails innovation, uplifting behavior, and highlights the Sinker mentality.

No Rush To Return To Communal Living

07:21 For the early humans a communal life was the only means for survival. The **interdependence** fostered many human developments such as tool making and verbal communication. The understanding early humans had and built upon regarding self and love of others was only developable within the communal setting.

07:22 If the benefits of individuality were comprehended before the viability to engage individualism was had, much needed communal development would have been lost, and potentially humanity in the balance. Once the necessity for communal life lessened, individuals could take their place as **leaders, innovators,** and **inspirations** for future generations.

07:23 Humanity is in a cycle that waxes and wanes between communal existence and individual expression. This is most likely a multi-thousand year cycle. In the distant past communal life was essential. The onset of the benefits of individualism was a **steppingstone** to the present. Where we are in this cycle can be debated.

07:24 The return to communal society will not come overnight as a sweeping edict handed down from governing hierarchies. It will be a gradual process and is probably thousands of years away.

07:25 When individualism no longer serves a greater purpose it will naturally diminish. The desire to skip portions of this cycle is detrimental and would eventually be found to be futile.

07:26 Humans do not pass through these phases as a **monolithic block of consciousness**. Some people are ahead of the curve and some are behind the curve. This is natural, flawless, and quite human. The insistence that one abandon their natural place in this process is unconscionable. The Total Sinker mentality wants to abandon individualism.

Individuality Continues From Creativity Into Conceptuality

07:27 The communal mindset excludes unnecessary **risk**. Interdependence overrules taking chances. This in turn precluded the potential rewards of chance discoveries. The risk-to-reward factor is a part of life. "Nothing ventured, nothing gained." At some point ancient man pushed the envelope. The **limitations** found in the security of a hunter/ gatherer clan were not satisfying enough. A daring and creative individual stepped forward to assert leadership. The risk was high and the reward was great.

07:28 Life is not directed as, **"evolution by committee."** Individualism was a bold step toward the expansion of humankind. Sufficiently resilient, chances could be taken and potential risk could be absorbed. The earliest of these leaders led their clan to more abundant hunting grounds securing the **prosperity** of future generations.

07:29 An individual became the proverbial spearhead and pierced the veil that separated the past from the future. Individualism has produced leaders in many forms. In successive generations leaders were militaristic, as well as, spiritual, intellectual, and cultural. Throughout time inspiration from individuals has propelled the upward movement of humankind, producing the growth and expansion of understanding between disparate cultures, and belief systems.

07:30 In recent millennia this evolution has continued. Yet what has remained relatively unchanged is an inherent human nature. At this point in time a part of human nature includes the Sinker mentality. This mindset is **arrogant, vain,** and **compulsive**. From a state of insecurity this personality type seeks to manipulate others.

07:31 Human nature also includes the Thinker mentality. This personality type is **calm, patient,** and **accepting**. This is the leader who does not first for themselves, but for the greater good. The one that does not seek the spotlight yet thoughtfully works to motivate others to do for themselves by creating, expressing, and sharing their experience. The Thinker knows that concepts shared draw us together. Equally understood is that we grow when we seek to communicate and understand others through our uniqueness and our commonalities. The Thinker mindset discards predetermined roles preferring the expressing of one's self within a code of **personal responsibility**.

07:32 The importance of having a moral code of behavior is far reaching. This moral code is established in accordance with **spiritual** and **religious** beliefs. It is set to create the best environment in which positive and uplifting behavior can be practiced and passed along. The adherent is directed to observe certain approaches and rituals yet largely this code delineates what the faithful must not do. Without knowing all the things that one might possibly do this is the best approach. Yet this moral code is something that is committed to **voluntarily**.

07:33 In a modern free society the rules established are more civil oriented. Here the rules are built to create a framework within which individuals may pursue their dreams and desires. This code establishes what is not allowed but also how the system must not infringe upon the freedoms of the individual. Here the framework calls less for the individual to perform certain actions instead defining how they will not be hindered on the path of their choosing. This leads to the **ultimate expression** of individuality.

07:34 The security of the communal life, with certain yet **limited rewards**, has been countered by the life of individualism with uncertain yet **unlimited rewards**. This culminates in the first modern **republic** where the Sinker has given way to the Thinker. This modern nation was where individuals took great risks throwing off suppressive governance for the uncertain yet greatest of rewards . . . **Liberty**.

07:35 Here the Sinker shutters while the Thinker sows the seeds of **opportunity,** not just for themselves but for all. This is a perilous proposition because human nature includes the Sinker mentality. This nature lurks in the heart of humankind searching for instances in which it can act to influence. **Jealous** and **narcissistic** the Sinker mentality postures in its ignorance of the possibilities of greatness. Substituting anger for acceptance it fails to rise. And in its arrogance it continues to seek to impose itself on others.

Chapter 8
Dynamic and Rigid
(Skimming the Surface)

08:01 The movement of matter through
time/space is a complex path.

08:02 The movement of matter through
time/space is of a dynamic and powerful nature.

08:03 Humankind is an extension of a
dynamic and intelligent nature.

08:04 To develop one's self
one must be thoughtful.

08:05 All natural movement is
due to the attraction of gravity.

08:06 Humans produce gravity
and are susceptible to gravity.

08:07 The more willing one is the more
possible they are able to connect with life.

08:08 We grow when we acknowledge,
appreciate, and remember.

08:09 The connection with our
dynamic nature can be developed.

08:10 Human imagination is a dynamic spark in life.

08:11 If one does not develop their
dynamic nature a rigid nature will appear.

08:12 Rigidity is the foretelling of failure.

08:13 Rigidity is the unwillingness or
inability to explore new ideas.

08:14 Swimming is a dynamic process.

08:15 If a swimmer (person), is rigid in
water (life), they will sink.

08:16 Love is dynamic; hate is rigid.

08:17 A rigid person is less able to
adjust to a dynamic world.

08:18 Rigidity is not uplifting.

Chapter 8
Dynamic and Rigid
(Entering the Waters)

- Life on earth is extremely dynamic. We choose how engaged we will be with this dynamic life.

- Our willingness to engage life draws us into a more dynamic life.

- When we withdraw from a dynamic life we become less dynamic and in result, rigid.

- Rigidity does not flow with events and possibilities.

- Love is dynamic. Judgment is rigid.

- When we choose between love and judgment we choose the life we will lead.

Chapter 8
Dynamic and Rigid
(Deeper Depths)

08:01 In the physical universe, all molecules and the atoms that constitute them vibrate. These particles are thought to move from point A to point B in a recognized path. Not only does the particle theoretically move back and forth but also the established path of the particle travels through time/space. First the path travels in a spiral as the earth revolves. Then again the path travels in a larger spiral as the earth orbits our Sun. And yet again the path of the vibrating particle travels an even larger spiral as our solar system orbits the center of our galaxy. Further the path of the particle once more travels a considerably larger path as our galaxy moves through the universe relative to time/space. These five discernible paths are actually perceivable sub-segments of one great path.

08:02 The underlying movement of the cosmos, on which all things balance, exemplifies our **dynamic nature**. This is represented in the Thinker - the character of activity and progress, a positive perspective with energy and productive ideas. The word, **"dynamic,"** comes from the Greek word meaning, "power." An essential part of nature is this dynamic power. This power is the inspiration for the Thinker mentality.

08:03 It is not a great leap to consider humankind being an extension of the essence of nature. Being a part of nature, humankind has access to this essential and dynamic power. Yet unlike the flow of water or the interconnected movement of astronomical bodies and structures, an individual possesses and can cultivate their connection to this essential power. On earth this ability is unique to humans as it is directly aligned with **intellect**.

08:04 The cultivation of self demands cognition, otherwise any improvement is along the lines of instinct which is devoid of intellect. The development of the connection between the essential nature of life and the human intellect is obtained through **attraction**.

08:05 In nature the movement of flowing water is created by gravity, which is a product of mass. This includes waterfalls, river movement, and the tides. Planets, solar systems, and galaxies were created, and, because of the mass in each, were drawn into motion by gravity. All matter has mass and is being drawn into movement by gravity. All things around us have mass and in so each has a gravitational field around it however small. There is no place near earth where there is no gravity. In what is called zero gravity there is still gravity. Even energy has mass. Mass equals gravity. Energy produces gravity.

08:06 Water splashes and objects bounce changing direction by storing and releasing **potential** and **kinetic energy**, but underlying all of this motion is gravity. Perspective will play with one's mind in this regard yet it is all about the attraction of gravity. As individuals, we are a part of this dynamic, and indeed hyper-dynamic universe. Everything in the universe, but most notably to us, humankind, is attracted to the great Spiritual Mass of our life and origin.

08:07 The level of our conscious connection to life is predicated on our personal ability, and/or willingness, to **acknowledge, appreciate,** and **develop** a connection to the environment and events of our experience. In this ability, and/or willingness, we decide how we will travel the path that results from the gravitational influences we encounter and create in life.

08:08 Humanity first acknowledged the natural wonders of our planet and the cosmos. We stood in awe and appreciation of the beauty and power of the world and universe around us. In turn we took from the resources and developed the standards of our condition and the conceptions of our mind. The process was not a straight line as we were attracted and influenced by the gravity of our surroundings. We grew **spiritually, physically,** and **intellectually**.

08:09   The wind blowing a pattern in a sand dune is natural. The situation and the creation of the pattern are **simple, beautiful,** and **dynamic**. But consider that same wind blown dune with the beautiful yet simple pattern and across it walks a scorpion, the dynamic level is heightened. The wind blowing, the rippling pattern on the dune is undulating but now with the appearance of the animated animal this scene provokes awe and excitement and power. This shows the levels to our dynamic nature. Which part we are in this scenario can be influenced by us, if we choose to acknowledge, appreciate, and develop our connection to the **Infinite Nature** that is the source of this dynamic life.

08:10   Now take a portion of that sand dune and put it into a low, open top, rectangular box. This is a common backyard item, a sandbox. Standing back and looking at the sandbox you see something lacking in dynamic character. It is a box with sand in it, which is not a big deal. What converts the sandbox into a dynamic device is when a powerful ingredient is added. That powerful ingredient is the **imagination** of a human.

08:11   Adding a person who is lacking in dynamic development changes little. The box and the person sit quietly, uninspired, and unexpressive. The potential is there because of the human. The actions needed to blossom and rise are not engaged. If unengaged the result is a rigid system destine to sink.

08:12   **Rigidity** is the foretelling of failure. Sometimes close inspection is needed to determine if a person, structure, or system is actually rigid. Stubbornness is not automatically a sign of rigidity. Stubbornness can be a sign of fortitude. It is important to realize what is being stubbornly withstood.

08:13   Rigidity is the inability or unwillingness to accept, or even explore, ideas that contradict beliefs held. If in a one-on-one setting, rigidity is easily overcome by **dynamism**. When the odds are more greatly in favor of rigidity, dynamism can be overwhelmed and suppressed. Rigidity produces less-able swimmers.

08:14   When a swim student enters the water for the first time their instructor will tell them to **relax**. This is essential in swimming - being comfortable is a positive way to invoke a dynamic process. Swimming is a dynamic process. The flowing movement of limbs, a calm breathing pattern, and positive mental posture contribute to swimming.

08:15   Newborn babies are **natural swimmers**. But if the swim student responds to the swim lesson in a rigid manner progress is impeded. Even simply performing the back float, one must be relaxed and dynamically engaged. If a swimmer were to hold their body stiff, in a rigid fashion, they would sink into the water. This rigid behavior carries over into other parts of life.

08:16   The rigidity of one's thoughts and actions returns commensurate fruit. **Love is dynamic**. Actions that lack love, often recognized as hatred, are rigid. Rigidity is found in the Sinker mentality. The Sinker is inflexible toward ideas contrary to their own. The limitation of possibilities in the mind of the Sinker produces an unyielding perspective to new ideas. Here the Sinker reveals the handles by which they can be manipulated. Their rigidity blocks reason from entering into their thought process.

08:17   The Sinker becomes fixed in their approach to life and less able to adjust to the dynamic world. This can manifest in the inability to cope with feelings of jealousy. A Sinker cannot admit to their shortcomings of **covetous behavior**. The dynamic response to feeling jealous is to use the feeling to positively achieve a goal. Rigidity demands possessions and produces distain for the perceived unfair reality of their want. Rigidity would seek to confiscate where dynamism would seek to multiply.

08:18 One nature is sinking, while the other is rising. The Sinker would **not be sated** by possessions. The proof for this is they continue to covet, they continue to be jealous, they continue to sink. If a Thinker loses possessions they will move forward in the manner that had delivered them to their previous satisfaction. They will work as they had before, they will innovate, they will rise.

Chapter 9
Nobility and Peasantry
(Skimming the Surface)

09:01 An evolving society creates
dynamic structures.

09:02 Nobility often reaped benefits
from efforts not their own.

09:03 Nobility were certain of their
importance based on lineage.

09:04 Nobility consumed refined art, science,
and philosophy disregarding its origin.

09:05 Society as a whole benefits
before the lower class.

09:06 Nobility gave something for
the lower class to strive toward.

09:07 Lifting the nobility higher eventually
drew the lower class upward.

09:08 Society and humanity
are made of all people.

09:09 Hard work eventually
brings benefits.

09:10 Fulfillment is not
predicated on class.

09:11 Having only a little money,
a person can still be spiritually rich.

09:12 With a lot of money, a person
can possibly be spiritually poor.

09:13 In life we do not choose who we are,
but how we will respond to who we are.

09:14 Class warfare persists thoughtlessly.

09:15 Class reflects
conditions one is born into.

09:16 In an evolved society,
classes can be traversed.

Chapter 9
Nobility and Peasantry
(Entering the Waters)

- The ruling class and elite have been part of society for a very long time.

- Being part of a dynamic system, change to any class structure is unavoidable.

- As people become more aware of the possibilities and their potential, the ruling class becomes less useful.

- When the elitist (Sinkers), in the ruling class, and those wishing to be, feel a diminishing sense of control they will seek to regain prominence.

- The friction between classes is used to divide opposition to the elite.

- Class is merely a starting point.

- One's social standing does not dictate if one is loving or judgmental, the individual makes that choice and the proof is in their behavior.

Chapter 9
Nobility and Peasantry
(Deeper Depths)

09:01 As society evolved dynamic structures took shape. The dynamism created was to foster **productivity**. The benefits of these systems were enjoyed first by those at the top of the system, then by the system, and lastly by those at the bottom of the system. Each facet was perpetuated, but because the system was part of a dynamic structure the underlying purpose and value of each was changing. What each enjoyed was a matter of perspective.

09:02 **Nobility**, those at the top of the system, reaped the benefits of human efforts that were not their own. Farming and militarism were the most recognized of these efforts. Every other manner of craft, science, and service were included.

09:03 The nobility were certain of their importance based primarily on lineage. Often the focused energy in the nobility was an accumulation of centuries of refinement, education, and breeding. In the distant past what separated the top of society from the bottom was small bits of knowledge. To perpetuate this the best of the best were combined to produce even more noble offspring. This is a continuing belief held in the Sinker mentality.

09:04 The nobility, in their **elitism**, nearly cornered the market on the production and possession of works of art, science, and philosophy. Though the source of these materials were far from exclusively nobles. This fact reveals the dynamism of the human condition. The nobility breathed contempt for those less sophisticated then themselves. They regarded the surface differences in a rigid manner that obscured the potential of the assumed lesser peasantry. Of course this did not precisely include the artists, scientists, or philosophers of lower class origins who had been examined and whose talents had been discerned. The prejudice the nobles held was not reserved for the lower class.

09:05 The **societal structure** also benefited from the dynamic formation of the class system. To sustain the fertile beds of human development the class system subjugated many and poured resources into the few. This crude distillation process worked to purify society. The shortcomings of which were never seen approaching.

09:06 As the nobility became more polished so did the lower class. Obvious, proof for this is found in what has become known as the middle class. This middle class is recognizable as more refined than the lower class yet certainly not nobility. Society sacrificed the many to produce the ideal standard of living . . . the nobility. The nobles were the example toward which the lower class could strive in becoming, **"more human."**

09:07 The focused and perfected lives of the nobles lifted a society up from the simple origins of the group. In this endeavor countless advances in the human condition, both materially and philosophically, were achieved. The desire to understand greater things in science, psychology, and consciousness were approached. All this was possible because while most endlessly toiled the few were shaped by **fine-tuned stimuli**.

09:08 Yet in this approach nobility and society at large lost touch with the fact that society and humanity consist of all people. The lacking memory of this reinforced over centuries formed callous disregard for the pedestals upon which the nobles were raised. For without the peasants the nobles stand upon the same ground as the peasantry, and left to their own devices many would revert to earlier forms if not simply perish.

09:09 Lastly, the **peasants** benefited. Though none would cast off later comforts for the good ol' days of living in a sod hut, the burden was shouldered for the sake of future generations. Through unrelenting hardship the lower class strove to lift themselves from dirt floors to less modest yet still impoverished settings. Some attained greater success than others, but still most labored without end.

09:10   Many of the pursuits of the lower class demanded some level of competence. Farming, manufacturing, and animal husbandry had simple beginnings but soon revealed the requirements of greater understanding to achieve greater production and quality. The pride developed, earned, and felt was as great as any other achievement of humankind. Found in an individual life, the fulfillment of purpose grants to all a unique value. This sentiment overlooked by nobility, and society at large, discards the essential values of the human spirit, deeming more worthy appearances over **essential substance**.

09:11   The mindset of the Thinker and the Sinker are easily identified within the nobility and peasantry paradigms. Understandably each is found in both extremes. The nobles who reached for greater **understanding** of life and purpose and the peasants who exerted themselves as the **building blocks** of society were both exhibiting the Thinker mentality.

09:12   The nobles who believed themselves to somehow be **better than others** and the peasants who **bemoaned** their lot as futile were both exhibiting the Sinker mentality. All these years later, little has changed. The choices of actions in response to conditions remain.

09:13   **Opportunities** affording one comfort and enlightenment can be taken advantage of. Task that impose individuals to periods, if not whole lives, of less-desirable conditions are endured. While special moments are savored and grand meanings are looked passed; personal authenticity is embraced and personalities are contrived; fates are shouldered and responsibilities are fled from. This has and, for the foreseeable future, will continue across the spectrum of human experience. In this life we do not choose who we are, yet we choose how we will respond to who we are, which can lead to who we become.

09:14 The Sinker mentality inflames the **friction** felt between the classes. Thinkers assess themselves and their situation and in the acceptor mold move forward to achieve. The class warfare struggle that persist is occasionally reinvigorated as a necessary part of the Sinker mentality.

09:15 **Propaganda** must be reinforced on a daily basis to prevent logic from taking hold. What separates the classes is less important than what all people have in common. Someone with reason and industry will harness their efforts to improve their conditions. Someone who is combative and thoughtless will deny facts standing directly in front of him or her. What separates the classes has nothing to do with who is a Thinker and who is a Sinker. The classes largely reflect the conditions one was born into.

09:16 In accommodating societies, classes can be traversed. The classes need not be mutually exclusive and to the Thinker are inconsequential as to the individual's worth. Pitting these groups against each other is nothing short of a belligerent war brought about by the **fearful, unhealthy,** and **ingrate** perspective of the Sinker.

Thinkers

trending upward

PRINCIPLED

self-assured

sensible

accepting

grateful

happy

rational

composed

thoughtful

wise

gracious

patient

CIVIL

empathetic

polite

calmly skeptical

law-abiding

INTROSPECTIVE

cognizant

SINKERS

trending downward

thoughtless judgmental

ARROGANT

angry ingrate

suspicious

scornful

coercive

shrill

vain

jealous obsessive

clamorous

mean combative

impulsive

criminal narcissistic

UNBALANCED

ILL-MANNERED

Chapter 10
Good and Bad
(Skimming the Surface)

10:01 Wars begin because of
belligerent behavior.

                        10:02 An intent belligerent
                        cannot be avoided forever.

10:03 War is not an argument, but
behavior intent on death and dismay.

                        10:04 Death is the end of
                        a human life.

10:05 War is also used
to spiritually kill.

                        10:06 War is larger than conflict.

10:07 War is larger than contest.

                        10:08 Conflict and contest
                        need not become war.

10:09 The makers of war
first make conflict.

10:10 Before war is made
support is sought.

10:11 The makers of war
are easily seen.

10:12 If the people do not attend
to society, war is made.

10:13 The makers of war will first
seek to misguide the public.

10:14 Wisely identifying and
dealing with conflict is important.

10:15 We are a reflection of the
value of our endeavors.

Chapter 10
Good and Bad
(Entering the Waters)

- When people, nations, or ideologies interact behavioral choices are made.

- Those hoping to dominate others use belligerent characteristics.

- In a modern world when faced with a domineering person, nation, or ideology running away will likely only delay their desire to dominate. If the target does not fight back they will be overcome.

- Being clear as to the motives of others is very important. Understanding one's own motives is equally important.

- We embody the values we hold.

Chapter 10
Good and Bad
(Deeper Depths)

10:01 If war is bad then both parties engaged in the conflagration are acting with ill-intent. More likely one of the participant parties is behaving **belligerently** and the other is responding out of **self-preservation**, which is also known as, survival.

10:02 There is a basic survival response found in humans, and animals, known as the **fight-or-flight response**. This works well in the wild. But on a global field where nations, or consolidated ideologies, can reach hundreds of miles or around the globe, the flight portion of fight-or-flight will only forestall the desires of belligerent intent. Those who wish to mitigate the belligerent behavior may say those behaviors stem from self-preservationist wants. When this is not the case these are not difficult concepts to disprove.

10:03 If a war is launched with belligerent intent then reversing or destroying of those desires is noble and yes in a word, just. The reason behind the necessity for destroying the belligerent war behavior is what it will inevitably produce. Belligerent **war behavior** by design brings about death and dismay.

10:04 **Death** eliminates further expressions of human life by those who have been rendered dead. Expressions of life include: creations of art, care and comfort of another human being, and the development of ideas. If one were to look at the history of humanity one would see these expressions in abundance throughout the ages. This is because this is what uplifted people do.

10:05 Other products of belligerent war are destruction and **dismay**. Dismay, defined by consternation and distress within the spiritual heart and mind, produces, in degrees of totality, everything that death produces, yet the physical body continues to function. The experience had through death, dismay, and destruction constricts still living individuals affected by the events. Beyond death, dismay is another way of killing. What is killed is the **human spirit**.

10:06 **War** has often been characterized as **conflict**. Yet this word play goes a long way to excuse belligerent actors. Conflict is a much simpler and less-destructive effect. Although considered serious the range of conflict extends to things that clash. Ideas that are incompatible are said to conflict. Colors that do not match or harmonize clash and therein conflict.

10:07 A person is **conflicted** when what they are presented with is not consistent with the belief system they have developed for themselves. Going back to the Latin word **"conflictus"** we find a definition indicating contest. Anyone who would call a war a contest is dangerously disregarding the gravity consigned in the outcome of war.

10:08 Conflict between peoples and ideas can actually produce positive benefits. This all rest upon the honest and thoughtful reflection given to conflicting matters. To achieve this end, necessary levels of awareness and intellect are required. More importantly, conflict need not rise to the level of war and the **deleterious** results sought through belligerent behavior.

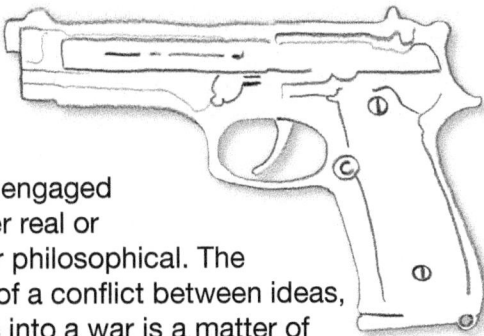

10:09 Before war is engaged conflict exist, whether real or imagined, physical or philosophical. The belligerent elevation of a conflict between ideas, standards, or desires into a war is a matter of choice. Many belligerent actors work to fabricate a conflict as to **facilitate** a belligerent war with aims on gain.

10:10 In personal and public affairs this holds equally true. To gain desires often sides must be drawn and support must be acquired to justify purpose, if only for effect, and

to catalyze action for manifesting the goal. Any belligerent party that acts alone will likely face a reduced rate of success if they have not openly stated a case and gathered support, however and from wherever, before acting.

10:11   To any degree the true motives are openly stated, a belligerent actor will be revealed. Revelations usually come long after events have been put into motion. Belligerent actors always seek to bring about conflict. This is often designed to **degenerate into war** of some kind.

10:12   What words are used to lull support from the uninformed are naked and when viewed in the light of logic can be seen for the propaganda that they are. How easily and clearly **rhetoric** is disassembled is the result of experienced minds. This will be matched by the experienced minds that first assemble the words that were designed to mislead. And in the middle, the body that holds the most power over events, the masses.

10:13   If the public is **persuaded**, policy and action moves in the direction of its leaning. If the public is misled matters not in the short run. The belligerent actor seeks to create conflict and discord. This can be all the bad actor is hoping for to attempt its goal. These goals will fail, and there will be **consequences**, as we will see later in this manuscript.

10:14   How one identifies and deals with conflict is both valuable and important. **Valuable** because if one properly resist tagging situations, people, and events as sources of conflict - time, effort, and dealings with the repercussions of such action will all be spared availing the individual with more opportunity to realize their greatest potential.

10:15   When we consistently engage in behavior that has little worth we reduce our potential. When we limit our engagement with what produces little or nothing we increase our potential. Knowing the difference is not that difficult. Though properly identifying these actions is **important**.

Chapter 11

Discernment and Judgment
(Skimming the Surface)

11:01 Wisdom and knowledge are
two entirely different things.

11:02 Judgment is one
person's decision for all people.

11:03 Discernment is one
person's decision for themselves.

11:04 Murder has been judged,
for all people, to not be good.

11:05 In free societies religious
beliefs do not influence all civil laws.

11:06 Making laws has long
been a part of human life.

11:07 Social morals and criminal
law are not always connected.

11:08 When someone decides
for another they judge.

11:09 Judging others can create friction.

11:10 People will want others to follow them.

11:11 People judge in an attempt
to make themselves feel secure.

11:12 Determining for others outside a
civil framework is potentially flawed.

11:13 Discerning for one's
self is self-expression.

11:14 One can create wisdom for
themselves through self-expression.

11:15 The conflicts of judgment persist.

11:16 Being judged can
easily lead to judging others.

11:17 Not considering ideas or
criticism requires no thought.

Chapter 11
Discernment and Judgment
(Entering the Waters)

- Wisdom and knowledge are not the same.

- Determining for one's self is different than determining for others.

- As we grow in self-awareness we must be allowed to make determinations regarding ourselves. Self-determination is how we achieve our greatest personal goals.

- Outside of civil laws, and for the foreseeable future, there will be people who will want to tell others what they may and may not do.

- Until people stop telling others what to do in their personal and social life, friction will persist.

Chapter 11
Discernment and Judgment
(Deeper Depths)

11:01   One can only ever speak, with **wisdom**, from their experience. The wisdom of one may be passed to another but without the first-hand experience, close observation, and sufficient reflection what was wisdom reverts to knowledge. Only when knowledge is experienced first-hand, closely observed, and sufficiently reflected upon can it become wisdom, yet only then within the mind in which the transformation took place.

11:02   **Judgment** must not be confused with **discernment**. Some will quibble that this is semantics. For this discussion, and to illustrate a point, let us approach it as if it is not. The latter, regardless of foundation, is the understanding in quality between, "good for me," and, "not good for me." The former is an actual determination of quality pertaining to gross values applied en mass.

11:03   The actions taken as **discernment** are a direct result of an individual choosing between, "this is good for me," or "this is not good for me." The actions taken under **judgment** are a direct result of determining, "this is good for everyone," or, "this is not good for anyone."

11:04   Hence judgment is an expansive determination effecting all regardless of the discernment of an individual. Point in case: **murder** has been judged not good for anyone. Regardless of how an individual may feel about murder criminal law reflects the determination that for the individual, as a point of law, murder is not good for anyone.

11:05 The judgment of some matters has been carried over from criminal law to the larger arena of social behavior. In free societies large swaths of social behavior are not subjects of criminal laws. Matters have been determined to be not good for anyone by concerned citizens, yet this has been done disregarding individual discernment. These instances mainly include matters deemed important in **religious adherence** but that no longer draw the attention of criminal lawmakers such as the eating of a particular diet, daily, weekly, or annual prayer rites, and other traditions, morals, and values.

11:06 The **arbitration of social behavior** has been with humankind for a very long time. The system for adjudication was set in the earliest power structures. Commonly, the judge has been a tribal elder, a community counsel, or other, sometime self-appointed authority.

11:07 In the present and in republics and democracies the source of **criminal law** is well defined. The source of social morals is more loosely determined. Within the framework of liberty, individuals decide for themselves what social code they wish to align with. When discernment has been applied, and the choice made, the obligatory submission to the code is implemented. Here is where things get interesting.

11:08 When a group determines that it would be good for everyone, including individuals outside their social set, to adhere to the code of the group, a judgment has taken place **superseding** the discernment of the individuals who have not chosen to belong to the aforementioned group.

11:09 When this occurs friction is most likely to be created. This can come about in a variety of ways. Commonly, a group will determine the superiority of their social code and wish that the code would be adhered to by the **non-compliant**.

11:10 More commonly, an individual will determine the superiority of their personal choice in social or religious conduct. Adhering to the chosen code, and with pronounced determination, they seek another to follow suit. This seeking of others to comply with a particular code may be propelled by at least two simple motives and a third overarching motive.

11:11 **First**, the desire of the persuader to see the non-compliant secured in the safety the first has found within the social code. **Second**, the persuader, reflecting their choice to submit to a chosen code, will seek to eliminate, within their abilities, behavior outside their chosen code thus securing themselves and their choice. A **third** and overarching motive is to exert control to manipulate expression and individual fulfillment in the desire to dispirit. This is pursued to assuage perceived personal shortcomings, to deny reality, and to eschew personal responsibility. Here we see the undermining of the Thinker mindset and the supporting of the Sinker mindset. This is the goal of all who are dominated by the Sinker mentality.

11:12 In the first two instances a judgment has been reached determining that the chosen code is good for everyone regardless of the discernment of the non-compliant and the lack of criminal law determining so. In the case of the third instance belligerent motives are revealed as part of the most destructive aspect of current human nature, the Sinker mentality. Seeking to alter the **behavior** of others, outside of a civil framework, is potentially flawed.

11:13 Determining for another **self-realizing** and **self-determining** individual leads to discord and the frustration of individual growth. The expression of the self is the out forming of the relationship one has with life. Notwithstanding unintelligent choices, people live to express themselves through **acts of creativity**.

11:14 Only through the first-hand experience, close observation, and sufficient reflection of one's behavior can the greatest understanding and wisdom arise. Civilized societies act to pass into law codes protecting the population against behaviors judged to be not good for anyone. Members of these civilized societies choose to remain part of those societies and insofar imply adherence to criminal law determined.

11:15 The conflicts of judgment persist. **Unaffiliated individuals** or members of a particular group may wish to see non-compliant members of society adhere to their chosen code. The individual outside this group or apart from the formerly mentioned individuals discerns that the code they have chosen for themselves is good for them.

11:16 Quite naturally, and quite often, the non-compliant individual creates judgment on their own account by making determinations regarding the behavior of the group or individual that sought their compliance. Both parties seek change outside of themselves when if both parties sought awareness within themselves each would express themselves in accordance with criminal law and the wisdom of their life experience.

11:17 The **proselytizing** for conversion to any belief system can be discerned as non-judgmental if the persuader offers their opinion without demand of conversion. If a potential convert has been approached and offered concepts and they do not consider the concepts, discernment has not occurred. Either a judgment of, "this is not good for anyone," has occurred or no thought has been given. Instincts do not engage cognition to discern if a concept is worthy of adoption or not. Yet with the myriad possibilities found in cultures, traditions, and habits from around the world not every instance can be afforded great in-depth deliberation. Here our tuned and developed intuition can highlight, from a perspective of neutrality, what, for whatever reason, is advantageous for exploration. In the end, discernment, judgment, instinct, or intuitive response regarding the concept is our choice. What is attached to these forms of response will lead the individual in a direction forming behaviors that will likely have **enduring influence**.

The **Total Sinker mentality** is enveloped in darkness, is sinister, and in a word, evil. Among all the forms assumed by the Sinker mentality, the grip of enslavement is never far from view. If not actually being physically imposed with chains and shackles, the emotional and spiritual equivalent is employed. To that end the goal of utter destruction lays in wait for humanity. **President Abraham Lincoln** spoke of a national struggle with human slavery and could have easily been speaking of all humanity when he said, "A house divided against itself cannot stand."

His sentiments seem to say: "Humanity cannot endure forever half slave and half free. Humanity will not disappear from the face of the earth and as it will remain whole it will become all one thing or all the other." All Sinker or all Thinker. "As this House of Humanity is divided upon itself - a foundation is set for the Sinker to build their hopes of subduing the Thinker." Only through the insidious actions of the Sinker can this happen. Through these actions the thoughtful would be eroded until overcome by the thoughtless and plunged into the all-consuming pit of the Sinker mentality. This would be a slavery so complete as to be **bereft of peace**.

Chapter 12
Right and Might
(Skimming the Surface)

12:01 Everyone understands
the idea of authority.

12:02 Since early history someone has
always been in the role of the authority.

12:03 Authority comes
with a title and a rank.

12:04 In the past everyone
knew where he or she fit in
the power structure of society.

12:05 In the past the power structure
of society was constantly reinforced.

12:06 In the past aligning one's
self with GOD was a path to authority.

12:07 Families often have a
power structure and authorities.

12:08 People follow others for reasons
that are proper or to avoid
coercive repercussions.

12:09 Might is the source of
coercive repercussions.

12:10 If Might is used it will
be needed again and again.

12:11 Unchallenging responses to and
repeated use of Might reveals insecurities.

12:12 Might is used to harass,
intimidate, and oppress.

12:13 The only valuable response
to Might is Righteousness.

12:14 Uplifting behavior is
found in Righteousness.

12:15 Righteousness is the foundation
of wisdom, justice, and love.

12:16 Might cannot defeat Righteousness.

12:17 Righteousness is constructive.

12:18 If the mind is not
engaged success is unlikely.

12:19 Righteous concepts can
remove destructive potential.

12:20 Righteousness asserts the
pursuit of Life, Liberty, and Property.

12:21 Advantages are found when
people live a life of Righteousness.

12:22 If we choose Righteousness,
Might will diminish.

Chapter 12
Right and Might
(Entering the Waters)

- Power and control structures are everywhere.

- Authority is necessary for productive civil structures.

- Often positions of authority are sought to control groups.

- Uplifting principles are a unifying foundation for humanity.

- Those who seek unprincipled control of society most often do so using coercion and deceit.

- However long it takes, the unprincipled will be replaced by the principled.

Chapter 12
Right and Might
(Deeper Depths)

12:01   The idea of **authority** is firmly grasped by humanity. There has always been a hierarchy in life. By definition this structure radiates from the top down.

12:02   It is thought that with few exceptions, in prehistoric times the **dominant male** led the family group. Times changed and the clan elders assumed leadership. As societies evolved so did the posturing of those who sought control and leadership positions over ever-expanding groups.

12:03   To lead, those at the top of these structures assumed a title, among which are; **Pharaoh, King, Sovereign, Emperor, Caesar, Czar,** and **Lord**. So the hierarchy might look like this - king, nobles, town elders, professional class, merchant class, laborer class, and lastly women and children.

12:04   This structure was in place and everyone knew where he or she fit. Many had no hope of ever improving their position. A merchant was never going to become the king and a laborer was not going to be nobility. For accepted reasons these were **worlds separated**.

12:05   Everyday the ideals and purpose for this structure were reinforced. Each level wields authority granted to it by virtue of intelligence, possession of preferred knowledge, or sheer right by essence of lineage. This authority extended to the lower levels where rights were few or nonexistent, while social orders prevailed from top to bottom.

12:06   To solidify the top spot, kings have proclaimed legitimacy because of their being a direct descendent of **GOD**. Others have claimed to be ordained by GOD. Most people understand the authority of GOD. If one could be convincing in their claim to speak on behalf of GOD they gained status and authority. Established royal families needed little more than to point to their progenitors to claim their rights.

12:07 Away from the structures of nations, states, and communities a hierarchy still comes into play. The family has a similar structure. At the top is the **authority** of the parent, however the adults agree to align this authority. Then naturally the pecking order usually runs along the lines of age from eldest to youngest. For some this carries on throughout their lifetime.

12:08 What motivates anyone to follow the instructions of another can be divided into two categories, **Right** and **Might**. The difference is day and night. Right has the quality of **Righteousness**. Might is characterized by **forcefulness**.

12:09 **Might** is the pressure brought to bear when an object, condition, or person(s) is physically unmovable and, barring coercion, **cannot be persuaded by logic**. Any thing, event, or population that is difficult to move in a desired direction will need outside impetus. If Might is employed once, it will need to be employed every time movement is desired even if it is merely the threat of the forceful persuasion.

12:10 Furthermore, in dealing with people, Might is the approach that must be applied on a daily basis to **coerce** compliance. The successful use of Might reveals the influential mindset of the Sinker mentality.

12:11 Both those applying Might and those that repeatedly respond in a satisfactory manner, to those applying Might, do so from the Sinker perspective. The simple fact of someone feeling the overt need to pressure another to fulfill their desire, and those acting in compliance so as to avoid an unpleasant response, reveals the Sinker within.

12:12 **Harassment, intimidation,** and **oppression** are all forms of Might. When Might is called upon to achieve goals those subjected to these treatments will either comply or stand to defeat the Sinker's forceful imposition.

12:13   The Thinker will recognize these demands as serious life threatening actions, and will move to end the behavior. The only valuable response to Might is Righteousness.

12:14   **Righteousness** is the immutable truth found in concepts that inspire uplifting behavior. Among these are phrases and single word ideals that communicate volumes of information. The Thinker mentality understands **Freedom**.

12:15   The mere mention of these words can fuel conversation for hours. Books have been written on the one-word belief system of Freedom. The uplifting energy in the concepts of **Wisdom, Justice,** and **Love** are all founded on Righteousness.

12:16   The Thinker respects and extols the **accepting nature** of actions supported by Righteousness. No one using Might will be able to defeat an ideal created from Righteousness. In the final analysis Truth always wins. **Deception** is always found out. Sinker perspectives rooted in time may add confusion to outcomes in contention yet in time Righteousness rises and the forcefulness of Might sinks.

12:17   **Self-pride** lacks Righteousness. Being Righteous, without judging, will inspire the marginal Sinker to forgo the use of Might. But this is not a call for passivity. The Total Sinker will not be dissuaded. Being Righteous is proactive where the focus is on building up and not tearing down - discerning for oneself expansive behavior over a destructive mindset.

12:18   In any physical endeavor genetics plays a powerful role, yet mental contributions ought not be overlooked. If the body is capable but the mind is not engaged success is unlikely. The mental employment of **Righteous ideals** can overcome belief systems based in **hopelessness, anger,** and **humiliation**. The Sinker mentality can be assuaged.

12:19 The complete adoption of uplifting Righteous concepts can remove the destructive potential of **anger, fear,** and **self-pride**. Understanding the foundation of one's actions gives insight to the spiritual support they will have in their expressions of self. Knowing the solidity of Righteous based positions and the weakness inherent in Might provides foresight for choosing future actions.

12:20 As beings capable of intellectual thought, responsibility has been fought for on our behalf. **The Freeman** of the late 1700s risked everything they had and the future of their families and their associations to assert the Righteousness of **Life, Liberty,** and **Property**.

12:21 To best take advantage of this opportunity these thoughtful individuals called for all people to live **a life of Righteousness** - to embrace a way of life that is thoughtful. Righteousness and Might may appear to be a case of duality yet is more specifically an instance of **polarity**.

12:22 In our behavior we may think and act on varying levels of Righteousness until we sink to behavior that more represents Might. In deferring to our instincts we are not engaged in the process. If thoughtful to any degree we will choose how much Righteousness is contained in our thoughts and actions. When the **behavioral characteristic** of Righteousness is not present Might will be close at hand.

Chapter 13
Polarity and Duality
(Skimming the Surface)

13:01 A symbol from ancient China, the
Yin/Yang, illustrates opposites.

13:02 The Yin/Yang represents
opposites, as well as, the
opposites in each opposite.

13:03 Over time most things
reveal the opposite from within.

13:04 Some opposites are
masculine/feminine,
aggressive/passive,
and logical/emotional.

13:05 Hot and cold are two
places on the scale of temperature.

13:06 The spectrum of polarity
can connect seeming opposites.

13:07 On the scale of temperature there
are many points between hot and cold.

13:08 Perceiving subtle differences on the
scale of human behavior is challenging.

13:09 Good and evil are
differing degrees of one thing.

13:10 What makes someone
good can vary between people.

13:11 What makes someone good
or evil can be of a slight difference.

13:12 One act can
label someone evil.

13:13 The Sinker mentality needs
there to be winners and losers.

Chapter 13
Polarity and Duality
(Entering the Waters)

- Opposites appear all around us. Yet upon a closer look connections between opposites can be found.

- In the final analysis it is realized that seeming opposites are actually facets of a single thing.

- The difference between opposing objects, situations, and people may appear vast or small.

- When explored it is found that the distance between the opposites is actually traversable.

- Those that hold to the concept of opposites most often do so for the purpose of manipulation of themselves and others.

Chapter 13
Polarity and Duality
(Deeper Depths)

13:01 To understand life and the universe in which they lived the people in the ancient lands of what is now China observed nature. In observing nature they developed the **Yin/Yang** symbol by mapping a shadow cast by the Sun. Over the course of a year the shadow traced an organic form. This symbol embodies the balance of strong and weak, day and night, hot and cold, and the like. In this symbol can be seen the physical separation of the **Thinker** and the **Sinker** - the uplifting and the suppressing traits found in human behavior.

13:02 The **world-recognized** symbol of duality, the Yin/Yang, has led to an understanding of the cycle of change. Within the portion representing summer, a marker was placed to denote the longest day of the year and the subsequent turn toward winter. Summer is the white portion and the black circle therein marks the shift. In the opposing portion, the winter solstice is marked with a white circle representing the turn toward summer.

13:03 The **philosophy** found in the symbol acknowledges the presence of each aspect in the other and the natural cycle of one leading to the other. One illustration would be a fissure in a giant block of granite. The granite block represents masculinity and strength while the fissure represents femininity and weakness. Other examples point to winter following summer, night following day, old age following youth. These are natural occurrences. When considered in the framework of humanity, life situations and emotions appear more complex yet generally the Yin/Yang still applies.

13:04 Humanity at large displays traits and **characteristics** comparable to the Yin/Yang. Some of these are masculine/ feminine, aggressive/passive, and logical/emotional. The philosophy of the Yin/Yang, while representing duality as two separate aspects, can also be viewed as one entity containing both opposites. Within polarity, a reasoning mind can connect the extremes of the spectrum into a single scale.

13:05 Hot and cold are not two different entities as much as they are two locations on the single spectrum of **temperature**. Introduce an outside action and one can convert an object that is cold to a state of being hot and vice versa. Duality treats these as two different things whereas polarity shows them as residing on a single spectrum in two places. Each of these locations is able to move to the location of the other on the **shared scale**. They are actually connected.

13:06 All human behavior is connected on a spectrum showing **polarity**. The give and take in society has provided us with competing perspectives that have been the foundation for our development - the fast paced lifestyle of city folk and the slow paced lifestyle of country folk; the dogmatism of zealotry and the freewheeling nature of the non-conformist; anarchy and totalitarian rule. As one gives way in their attitude, they begin to move toward the opposite end of the scale. In this concept it does not come down to whether a person is one thing or another but, more specifically, how much of one and/or the other.

13:07 On the scale of temperature, hot does not click over to cold at a particular point. Instead, **myriad increments** separate hot and cold. Warm is not hot and cool is not cold. Water can also be described as being lukewarm, frigid, and of scalding temperatures.

13:08 Because we have thermometers, we can establish 98.6 degrees as a normal internal temperature of the human body. Yet the running of hot and cold in human behavior is not as easily discerned. From our unique perspective we see generalities that we judge as reasonable and unreasonable, desirable and undesirable, moral and immoral. What this reflects is more about us than about what we are perceiving. We reveal where we are on the scale of acceptance by how we discern and how we choose to respond to non life-threatening instances in the world around us.

13:09 In the world of polarity, **good and evil** disappear as separate realities. Yet in the mind of the observer who understands polarity they will first ask if the scale is of goodness and the lack of goodness or evil and the lack of evil. Here we reveal ourselves again. The Thinker is focused on what makes them happiest. The Sinker is focused on what makes them saddest. The Thinker sees goodness and the Sinker sees evil.

13:10 Speaking of good and evil is **understandable shorthand**. But since this is a scale of human attention, there will be a point when good seems to click over to evil. There is a breaking point for us. We barely see something losing its goodness. We mostly see when it does not seem good anymore.

13:11 In the vagaries of human perspective, moving from a point of being good to a point of being evil is potentially half a step away. This determination is made in regard to any matter and qualifies the matter only in the mind of the observer. It may match the determination of others but remains qualified for the individual, by them, in their mind. We can influence others but only if they accept the influence and we cannot be influenced until we allow another's influence to take hold.

13:12 Becoming evil is as easy as performing a single act. Becoming good can be a lifetime travail when attempting to overcome one evil act, and still the actor may come up short.

13:13 In this case duality survives only in the mind of the individual who clings to its construct - the Sinker. In the world at large duality is dispelled forever if anyone can rationally hold a diametrically opposing perspective to another person. While polarity contains seeming opposite the ability to traverse perspectives reveals the unity in the subject matter even as diametrically opposing perspectives are held. This is because the opposing beliefs are founded on a scale of understanding that is traversable and while a person may change their perspective they do not change the possibilities within the spectrum. **Polarity becomes the norm** when a vast multitude of the population embraces the Thinker mindset believing everyone is capable of uplifting behavior. This would bode well for realizing that trend.

Note: A shared perspective is required in the duality that represents absolute separation of opposites. In the case of polarity what is, "desirable," is predicated on the individual's viewpoint and, therefore, cannot be contradicted without the imposed perspective of another. People who cling to duality do so to construct winners and losers, focusing on what is not desirable and hoping to impose their views on others. This supports their Sinker mindset. When duality is dispensed with, all things can have some desirability. If there were, in fact, a personality named the devil, the world of polarity would hold that this personage could attain redemption.

Chapter 14
Swimmers and Less-Abled Swimmers
(Skimming the Surface)

14:01 Life is like the passing river waters.

14:02 The River of Life moves us with purpose.

14:03 Being in the River of Life
calls for personal engagement.

14:04 The River of Life carries along
abled and less-abled swimmers.

14:05 For many the perceived inability
to live life reflects a momentary conception.

14:06 How well someone can swim will not
be known until they respond to the River of Life.

14:07 Events can often define an individual.

14:08 One can only learn to swim
by entering the waters.

14:09 Life threatening situations can
activate skill and/or a frantic response.

14:10 People have been drowning
since people began swimming.

Chapter 14
Swimmers and Less-Able Swimmers
(Entering the Waters)

- The metaphor of the River of Life calls us to action, moving us with purpose, and challenging us. Some will assume themselves unable to swim the River of Life.

- To survive in the River of Life, action must be taken. Some will rise to the challenge. Some will seek the willing or coerced help of others.

- In their time of need, people can discover skills they did not know they possessed.

Chapter 14
Swimmers and Less-Able Swimmers
(Deeper Depths)

14:01 Metaphors communicate vast quantities of information in very small packets. The idea that life is a flowing river has been used for millennia. The concept of time flowing by like the passing waters denotes the perceived fleeting nature of life. Understandably, the metaphor of an individual being a swimmer may come to mind.

14:02 In this illustration every person is within the life representing water. Within the currents of the water we can choose to move with the **currents of life** or struggle against them. This does not mean we docilely go wherever the currents take us, submitting to a capricious world, but that we appreciate where the currents are taking us and live through the purposeful events presented.

14:03 Being swept along by a moving current is **not an achievement**. Swimming is not a passive activity but one that requires the engagement of all muscles and may prove more beneficial with the deployment of the intellect.

14:04 Among the people in this **metaphoric river** there are those who can swim and those who are less-able swimmers. As time marches on the moving currents are sweeping all along.

14:05 Saying someone is a less-able swimmer is a momentary discernment. Saying someone can not swim is usually a determination presented more correctly in the past tense, as in rather they could not swim. We only really know if someone cannot keep their head above water **upon their drowning**.

14:06 For this metaphor the acceptor, the Thinker, is a swimmer, the judgmental, the Sinker, does not swim well or believes they cannot swim. **Polarity** shows everyone to possess some swimmer abilities. Who can swim and how well is sometimes a matter of perspective, obviously well sometimes, unexplainably poorly at others, and unexpectedly proficiently in a crisis. One may think of themselves as a swimmer with great ability until they are confronted by an event where their skill is truly tested. Then the realization of how well they can actually swim becomes clear.

14:07 Some may think of themselves as not a good swimmer yet they rise to the occasion to prove themselves deserving of the title. Events can often define an individual. An unprepared or **unsuspecting person** might fall into water thinking they are not a swimmer but to survive they must swim to some degree.

14:08 The muscle strength, poise, and coordination needed to swim can only be **learned in the water**. Until one gets wet they can only imagine what it means to swim. And once they get wet they can assess where they are in the flowing currents of life.

14:09 Here those who thought themselves less-able may **rise to the moment**. Events will spur some to swim while prompting others to seek survival in different ways. The emotion of an impending death can activate skill and/or a frantic response. There is no telling what will occur in the **River of Life**.

14:10 People have been swimming since **prehistoric times** and have probably been drowning just as long.

Chapter 14 - Swimmers and Less-Able Swimmers

Imagine the panicked swimmer **clawing** for support in the water as the unwitting rescue swimmer gets too close.

The Sinker is focused only on saving themselves. Then the rescue swimmer is **dehumanized** to the Sinker, appearing more like an outcropping of land or floatation device.

The rescuer's undoing is made whole as they lower their guard. The panicked swimmer climbs atop and drowns their would-be rescuer.

Identifying who is Sinker and who is Thinker is not always an easy task. Sinkers do not realize their **plight** and do not appreciate their opposite. Thinkers **underestimate** their mindset and overestimate their counterpart.

Chapter 15
Teaching Sinkers to Swim
(Skimming the Surface)

15:01 If a person struggles in the
water, and is to survive, someone
will have to do something.

15:02 Once in the River of Life
all preparations are past.

15:03 If a person struggles in
the water they will either drown,
save themselves, or be saved by another.

15:04 A person is always worth saving.

15:05 Risking life to save life
is a reasonable debate.

15:06 Some lifesaving attempts
may be beyond reason.

15:07 A person might have
abilities they do not suspect.

15:08 A person who is
thoughtful can find a solution.

15:09 Solutions often need to be
revised as new challenges arise.

15:10 Overcoming panic is no small task.

15:11 Emotion can bring on
thoughtless behavior.

15:12 Without thought, panic
can easily consume others.

15:13 Saving a person struggling
in the water can be treacherous.

15:14 The character and motives of an
uplifting person can inspire others.

15:15 A struggling person can
overwhelm an uplifting person.

15:16 To survive a life-threatening
situation, calm can help.

15:17 Calm can lead to clearer thought.

15:18 When receiving help,
cooperation smoothes the interplay.

15:19 A situation is not resolved until
it has been satisfactorily replaced.

15:20 To help another, a person will
sometimes enter into a dangerous situation.

15:21 Calmness, fortitude, and
focus can save a person's life.

15:22 Using the same reasoning
that got a person into an
unsettling situation is illogical.

15:23 Being thoughtful is a logical option.

Chapter 15
Teaching Sinkers to Swim
(Entering the Waters)

- Once we are born all preparations for life are past. Living life is about adapting to one's environment. This can include changing one's environment.

- Helping someone who is having trouble adapting can place the helper into unexpected circumstances.

- We all have the ability to rise to challenges.

- Reason, as opposed to emotion, more often holds better prospects for success.

- Uplifting behavior can inspire another to succeed.

- Being thoughtful leads in the direction of greater potential.

Chapter 15
Teaching Sinkers to Swim
(Deeper Depths)

15:01　There is someone in the water and they are struggling to keep their head above the **surface**. They are potentially in the process of drowning. The sounds of splashing water, calls of distress, and unintelligible words of panic can be heard. If someone does not do something this person will lose their life.

15:02　The person closes to this situation is the one most able to reverse this circumstance. That person is the one who is struggling in the water. It appears as though this person is incapable of saving their own life. The best time to change the potential of this scenario was before this person got in the water. Knowing how to swim would be a great skill to have before entering the water. Yet once in the water all preparations are **finished**.

15:03　There are three potential **developments** to this situation:

1. **The person drowns.**

2. **The person saves him or herself.**

3. **Someone else enters the scenario, and potentially the water, in an attempt to save the person.**

15:04　Allowing someone to drown is not an appealing choice. How the person has found him or herself in this situation is unknown. It may not have been their decision to enter the water. They may have thought they were prepared to swim, or their inability to swim may be a result of something beyond their control. Yet they are human and in so worthy of **saving**.

15:05   The value of human life is too great to allow to simply slip beneath the surface and being pulled down to a **watery grave**. Yet risking more life to save another life can make for anxious moments. Saving a panicked swimmer can be a treacherous undertaking. There are no guarantees when entering the water to life save.

15:06   Someone will have to decide if an attempt to save the life will be made. That also means the attempt may be deemed too risky. Which also means someone may be kept from making an attempt to save the life of the swimmer. Discernment may be made placing a value on the life of the struggling person and whether that person should be left to their own abilities **to fare as they might**. This potentially includes drowning. In which case, if they are to survive, the person may have to save themselves.

15:07   The possibilities of the unexpected may appear out of thin air. Humans are amazing beings. The resources at our command are mind-boggling. A flash of **insight, innovation, and inventiveness** has come at more unusual times, changing a person's life and lives of whole societies.

15:08   Consider a whole society backed against a proverbial wall by a massive empire that attempted to coerce their submission. These people were in way over their heads. Those who wanted to free themselves from this coercion, found for themselves the **will, skill,** and **direction** to rise to the top and make their way out of their freedom-threatening situation. The **American Revolution** may be the greatest example of this self-saving effort but all the others are equal in the sense that all others are facing the same certain death. Once found in this scene the swimmer will be called upon to overcome **hopelessness, fear,** and **despair** to preserve their life.

15:09   **The last option** is for someone to enter the water in an attempt to save the person. Pulling someone out of a drowning situation does not save his or her life permanently. It merely keeps the person from succumbing to the watery grave they were facing at that moment.

15:10 But saving a failing swimmer from certain death is more than just lending them a hand. With limited rescue tools the able swimmer must get close enough to the Sinker to calm them and recruit them into the effort to help save themselves. **Overcoming** the panic a Sinker feels is no small task.

15:11 When a person recognizes the possibility that their life may be at an unexpected end panic can set in quickly. Very likely they will act in thoughtless ways, flailing their body about in the water in a struggle to save themselves. The energy and **emotion** compacted in this action are off the scale of ordinary activity.

15:12 The sinking swimmer's instincts kick in and their **fight-or-flight** response creates great tension. This is the maelstrom the rescue swimmer enters. Without forethought a swimmer hoping to save a Sinker could become a victim of their own thoughtlessness.

15:13 **Lifeguard** courses will teach a rescue swimmer essential skills to save lives but more importantly to not become a casualty of their lifesaving efforts. A panicking person in the water will grab on to any object they think will buoy them in the water. This is generally done by climbing up on the object to get as much of their body out of the water as possible. This is not a problem unless the object they identify as their lifesaving last resort is the rescue swimmer.

15:14 Most equipped lifeguards will have some type of floatation device when they enter the water. This will likely be a small cylindrical buoy, often called a, "can," or a personal floatation device such as a, **"life ring."** The rescue swimmer will approach the Sinker in an attempt to save the person.

15:15 But before the floatation device can be personally delivered to the Sinker they must be calmed to some degree. There is a danger to the rescue swimmer if they get too close to the Sinker. The Sinker will prefer the help of a human to a floatation device. The rescue swimmer must communicate with the Sinker first.

15:16   A rescue swimmer might say, **"HEY! I'm going to help you but you have to calm down and relax so we can work together."** Anything can happen at this point but because the lifeguard is many feet away from the Sinker, panic may still reign in their mind. **"Hey! Relax! Calm down. Take it easy. You're going to be all right . . . take a big breath and let it out. Relax! Move your legs like you're riding a bike! . . . Relax!"**

15:17   If the **panic subsides** things are headed in the right direction, but anything can happen at any time. Panic can return without a seconds notice.

15:18   **"I'm going to give you this life ring, pull it under your chest and hang on to it. I have a rope attached to it and I'll begin pulling you to shore. If you feel like it, kick your feet. But if you start to pull on the rope I will take the ring away from you and you'll be right back where you are now. Do you understand?"**

15:19   This ordeal will not be defused until both are **buoyed, capably swimming,** or **on dry land**. The panicked swimmer wants reassurance that everything is going to work out and that they will get out of their situation. The rescue swimmer is there to help but they do not want to be overwhelmed by the Sinker. This could lead to tragedy.

15:20   Often the rescue swimmer has no personal floatation device and must save the Sinker by taking control of their body and pulling them to safety in close proximity. Here the panicked swimmer can easily reach the lifeguard and in their panic may attempt to buoy themselves using the lifeguard as a floatation device. The rescue swimmer can easily become overwhelmed by the panicked swimmer and become forced below the water surface. The rescue swimmer can be overpowered as the Sinker fights for their life. As the Sinker fights for their life the rescue swimmer may become **a drowning victim**.

15:21   The Sinker becomes overwrought by the possibility of losing their life. It is likely their **lack of awareness, emotionalism,** and **thoughtlessness** got them into their situation of peril. If they are to survive by their own hand their best option is to find the **calmness, fortitude,** and **focus** to do so.

15:22   If they are **lucky enough** to have someone come to their aid, and the person is capable of saving them, they will still need to cooperate to create a successful outcome. A Sinker will not survive if they employ more of the same thought process that got them into their life-threatening predicament. That approach is without sufficient thought.

15:23   Engaging the Thinker mentality offers the best option of extrication from the watery traps found in the fast moving currents of a river, whether it is the metaphoric **River of Life** or any other real body of water on this blue/green planet.

Note: Nowhere in this book, especially chapter 15, is meant to be instructive in actually rescuing a panicked swimmer. Life saving skills are applicable in many parts of life. Acquiring these skill should be sought from trained instructors. This book speaks metaphorically of a less-able swimmer to illustrate the irrational behavior of a person influenced by the Sinker mentality . . . nothing more, nothing less.

Chapter 16
Sinker Emotionalism
(Skimming the Surface)

16:01 When one is judgmental
they are dominated by emotion.

16:02 Being judgmental lacks
thoughtfulness and creates fear.

16:03 The judgmental will often
think, and pretend, they are exceptional.

16:04 The judgmental will
need to fight on to gain control.

16:05 The judgmental
will want endlessly.

16:06 A person controls themselves and,
at best, only influences otherwise.

16:07 The emotionalism of anger
usually produces nothing of value.

16:08 Anger can lead to a positive outcome
if it does not disable or destroy the individual.

16:09 A judgmental mind does not ask
questions with useful and uplifting answers.

16:10 Judgment breeds judgment.

16:11 Hope is available to all people.

16:12 At the depths of emotion the
options are death and surrender.

16:13 The end of a person's life is
not the end of their existence.

16:14 The judgmental can become accepting.

Chapter 16
Sinker Emotionalism
(Entering the Waters)

- Emotionalism is a fearful grip on life.

- When free flowing, emotions are not contrived. When counterproductive, emotions turn to being judgmental. Some emotions are real and uncontrollable. Some emotions are belief systems we have trained ourselves to accept, believe, and expect.

- Most often judgment brings more judgment.

- A person need not be manipulable and/or consumed by their emotions.

Chapter 16
Sinker Emotionalism
(Deeper Depths)

16:01 The **Sinker mentality** is dominated by dysfunctional emotions. The thoughts that consume the Sinker's attention are inwardly focused on themselves and a less-positive perception of life. The emotions the Sinker lives with are directed toward their feelings, mostly of what they perceived as having happened to them, or others, and the possibilities of these less-desirable things happening again.

16:02 This manner of behavior often thoughtlessly creates fear of the future. The focus of the Sinker is **egocentric**. All emotions are validation of the self regardless. The orgiastic and chaotic blend of Sinker emotions combines into a confusion that directs the Sinker's outcome.

16:03 A Sinker will first succumb to **self-pride**. This type of pride is destructive because it separates the individual into a world where they are pitted against the looming opposition to their beliefs. With self-pride a Sinker is commanded to muster courage to overcome their challenges.

16:04 Many think **courage** is a good thing. But the need for courage simply reveals the perception that there is something to fear. In this thought process one must have courage to rise above a situation. A situation that the Sinker believes must be conquered for their continuance. If they do not persist they feel they will lose control.

16:05 On their downward trend, **want** is the emotion that the Sinker becomes enveloped in next. Wanting to achieve a goal is purposeful but this is most powerful when the goal is realistic and can be thought of as already existing and/or in the process of materializing.

16:06 Goals that are wanted and not achieved create lack in the mind of the Sinker. Again they crave control, which is elusive because control outside of the individual is an illusion. This then spirals down leading into anger.

16:07   The **angry** Sinker is easily understood because what they want, and how they see themselves is not outwardly manifest. The emotionalism of anger produces nothing on a grand scale yet it can lead the Sinker into a stage of doing something to obtain a want. This can be uplifting if the action to obtain the desire is positive. If the action is not positive or short lived the upward movement and any positive growth stops.

16:08   When the growth stops, anger will soon be rejoined as material gains do not produce lasting satisfaction and will eventually give way to the lack embodied in unrealistic desires returning the Sinker to an angry disposition. This only leads deeper into an emotional state of **despair**.

16:09   To cope, important questions are not asked in the mind of the Sinker. Any encounters with salient thoughts fall uselessly into the mind pit of emotions where any answer the Sinker **contrives** is acceptable. But since the answers are egocentric in their structure, greater and ultimately more useful questions and answers are unlikely.

16:10   To the Sinker, feelings are less important than the simple fact that the feelings were had. This process opens the way to giving free reign to emotionalism which results in greater instability and more emotionalism which leads to the more deleterious emotions of **sorrow, remorse, hopelessness,** and **humiliation**. This is the pathway to the absolute bottom of the earthly emotionalist's existence.

16:11   Because we are all human and the human soul in the body is capable of, and is connected to, magnificent realities, **hope** maintains a supreme position in life. When the mind has sunk to a point of despair the body can take over.

16:12   **Instincts** motivate the body and direct events in two directions, downward into **utter destruction** or upward through **surrender**. At anytime a Sinker can surrender to that which is greater than the self. If not done consciously, the subconscious may necessitate a breakdown. A breakdown whether physical or mental is caused by exhaustion and can be a saving grace that can lead the Sinker into a position of accepting help to reorder their process. The Sinker mentality is not greater than the individual.

16:13 In some breakdown events the results are the death of the body. Yet as **life is eternal** the soul's journey continues. The separation of the soul and the body is a relief to the complete Sinker, as it will render them unto the larger spiritual mass of the Total Sinker mentality. This mass is not of the physical universe and is of a bittersweet comfort to the Sinker. Due to the nature of the human soul and spirit this person will once again rise to the physical universe to attempt another try at rising beyond it. This is our process.

16:14 Since the Sinker mentality is on the same scale as the Thinker mentality through thought and action it can move to where the Thinker can be found and where the inspiration of the Thinker mentality can be witnessed.

Chapter 17
Expendable Society Member
(Skimming the Surface)

17:01 To herd mentality,
individuality is a detriment.

17:02 The judgmental agree with,
yet do not care about each other.

17:03 Complaining is more about
complaining than doing anything positive.

17:04 Misery loves company.

17:05 Oppressive
personalities are judgmental.

17:06 Forcing strict conformity
on people is judgmental.

17:07 When complete conformity
is the goal, individualism is discarded.

17:08 If one person is deemed meaningless, any
person may be thought of as meaningless.

17:09 Oppressive organizations and oppressive
governments are run by oppressive people.

17:10 Oppressive people
deceive to ease their frailties.

17:11 Oppressive people inflict
might to demoralize others.

17:12 Ill-behavior toward
others is a cry for help.

17:13 Those that seek control over
others feel powerless over themselves.

17:14 Being oppressive
will not lead to happiness.

Chapter 17
Expendable Society Member
(Entering the Waters)

- Sinkers are drawn to conform with like-minded Sinkers where they commiserate with yet do not benefit each other.

- In creating complete conformity in society the oppressive work to manage the population into a single herd mindset.

- Where a single herd mindset is achieved the individual is devalued.

- The goal of the oppressive is control.

- All individuals, principles, and institutions are expendable when the oppressive seek authority.

Chapter 17
Expendable Society Member
(Deeper Depths)

17:01 The herd mentality, which is part of a dominate Sinker mentality, deals in terms of **suppression of individuality, complete conformity,** and the **collective**. Here the individual does not matter and is instead a detriment.

17:02 What matters is the **collective vibration** that matches the Sinker mentality. This self-supporting reality is an unchallenging emotional center shared by Sinkers yet attaches them to each other without real benefit to the individual. The benefit is instead to the Sinker mentality, perpetuating the continuance of the mutual despair experienced by those within it.

17:03 Perpetuating the Sinker mentality is the thoughtless goal of survival for the mindset. To maintain **despair** is to control the reality that the despair is legitimate. Regardless of why the individual Sinker despairs, they all count their sadness as **valid, important,** and **real**. In this case, if one Sinker were to disappear nothing in the Sinker mindset would change.

17:04 The Sinker feels camaraderie in those they **commiserate** with, yet do not recognize they are expendable to the others in the other's quest to express their unhappiness. A fallen comrade only validates the judgment of the Sinker. The vicious nature of this mindset is easily seen.

17:05 **Totalitarianism** is a celebrated form of governance among Total Sinkers. Here the dictatorial rule demands complete subservience. There is no space for individuality.

Individuality allows for value of one's thoughts and clarity in the understanding of personal worth and love. These are uplifting behaviors that are destructive to the Sinker.

17:06 **Depersonalizing humanity** is the first step toward destroying thoughtful behavior. The goal of justifying hopelessness sets into motion the rules for complete conformity. Conformity creates general controls by which all within the unit can be directed. This oppression disregards the individual and any singularly unique **thought, innovation,** and **contribution** of expression that does not first and foremost serve the direction of the oppressor/government. Individuals tend to fragment conformity and in that, the control sought by the self-appointed authority.

17:07 To assure the greatest success of **Sinker control,** a mutual goal is assumed which discounts the individuals in society. The mutual goal, spoken in unreal terms of making all persons the same, is fortified by vowing to achieve this goal by any means necessary. Seemingly presenting value for the individual this fully discards the individual.

17:08 **"The ends justify the means."** Here the ends are largely embraced though it is not likely understood to have different meanings to different people in the society. The expendable aspect of the society member comes into sharp focus at this point. The belief held is that one person's life is meaningless if the whole does not succeed. When this occurs that one person can be any person, or many persons. As this structure solidifies, much of the governed population becomes a floatation device for those controlling the masses.

17:09 At the top of a structure **predicated on the Sinker mentality**, by definition, Sinkers will be found. These individuals may not have yet sunk to the levels of total humiliation or sorrow but they are pointed in that direction. At the controls are more likely persons of great self-pride and persons who demand courage and sacrifice of others. These people are focused on what makes them saddest. They are arrogant, suspicious, angry, shrill, vain, and thoughtless individuals.

17:10 They have wrangled control of a society away from

the individual, and as all Sinkers do they attempt to create and perpetuate despair within the society. With blindness toward their **personal rage** they see no person having value other than themselves as they seek to assuage their emotional frailties through subjugation of others.

17:11 The illusion of Righteousness is pretended toward when all they are partaking of is the **infliction of Might** over demoralized humans. Humans that while in this structure have little or no hope of expressing who and what they understand themselves to be in their loving heart.

17:12 Consider what has been learned about **Totalitarian societies**. These are manifestations of the Sinker mentality. By attempting to replace the individual with nameless, faceless human robots - forced to live and labor in a setting without uplifting possibilities - the Sinker is appealing for help.

17:13 **They seek control** because they feel they have no control over themselves. They must combat the uplifting unity in the common bonds of **Love for Freedom, Nation,** and **Morality** found in a tapestry of communion and diversity. Their outward appearance of composure does little to quell the internal gnawing of insecurity that creates fear in their Sinker mindset.

17:14 Their inability to swim in the **River of Life** is seen in their unabated use of other human beings as floatation devices. And once one is drowned the more adept moves on to another leaving a trail of expendable society members in their wake. This behavior will only exacerbate the spirit of the perpetrator, as it is discomforting and antithetical to the expansive human nature.

Chapter 18
Thoughtful and Thoughtless
(Skimming the Surface)

18:01 At some time everyone
has had judgmental thoughts.

18:02 A judgmental thought
can illustrate how to be accepting.

18:03 With enough thought
we can answer any question.

18:04 Humans can reason with
intellect or act based on instinct.

18:05 When we act we can
use reason or instinct but not
both at the same time.

18:06 We develop our intellect
through knowledge, experience,
and reflection.

18:07 Instincts rules out a
reasoning thought process.

18:08 Instincts can be developed yet
when used there is no thought.

18:09 It is important to recognize
one's own intelligence and instincts.

18:10 Using intellect or instinct
at the appropriate time is important.

18:11 The ability to reason has lifted
humanity out of a primitive existence.

18:12 If intellect is called for
and instinct is used, current
knowledge is not applied.

18:13 Justifying emotions can
divert one's willingness to advance.

18:14 Thoughtfulness is the grand unifier.

18:15 Accepting that others have
their own belief system is intelligent.

18:16 Thoughtfulness is constructive,
honest, and accepting.

18:17 Thoughtlessness
produces whatever comes out.

Chapter 18
Thoughtful and Thoughtless
(Entering the Waters)

- At times every person has acted thoughtlessly.

- With thoughtfulness we can learn from our mistakes.

- In interpersonal relationships, being thoughtful is always an option.

- Instincts play a vital role in life yet are less important than one might think.

- While instincts have long been valued for survival, reason has brought about the most uplifting events known to humankind.

- Reason leads to the awesome.

Chapter 18
Thoughtful and Thoughtless
(Deeper Depths)

18:01 The Sinker mentality communicates experiences, such as **insecurity** or an **inflated self-pride**. All conscious humans have felt this. These emotions occur in a split second. These events can take hold and find accommodations within the frailties of the human condition. Frailties that are not inscribed upon the human soul and are not destine to prevail for all of time.

18:02 These frailties are lessons provided to instruct our greatest possible behavior, **The Power To Love**. Our navigation of this life is given to us in a supreme gift, **free will**. This is our ultimate right as we explore life.

18:03 As part of our connection to life, we come with a perspective by which we start our exploration. Within that perspective we have **answers** to every conceivable question. Even if we use one answer more than the others we respond to every inquiry and demand for action.

18:04 In our movement through life we choose from two repositories of options when we act. Our response to the world around us comes from **our mind** or **our gut**, in other words **our intellect** or **our instinct**. How we engage our mind for thoughtful guidance or allow our gut to direct us is our choice.

18:05 When we react to the world around us our **self-direction** comes from but one source at a time. If we rely on our intellect we block out our instinct. If we depend on our instinct we negate our intellect.

18:06 Over time we develop our intellect through **knowledge, experience,** and **reflection**. Our instincts may inform our mind and through this process we reason new understanding.

18:07 **Instinct**, by definition, rules out a reasoning thought process. We can develop our instincts yet when it is time to call upon this resource the innate nature found therein precludes cognitive efforts. This being the case when we act we are doing so exclusively through one attribute or the other - that is through our intellect or through our instinct.

18:08 One cannot act intellectually and instinctively at the same time. On a momentary basis we can engage in micro-behaviors that draw alternately from our instincts or our intellect. In the flow of life these actions may appear as a single effort but in fact they are a collection of actions streaming from different parts of our system. What aptitude one has in regards to these abilities is important to appreciate. How one decides which of the two resources is most useful and/or appropriate for any situation is potentially life altering.

18:09 Acting from instinct when intellect is demanded can change the course of one's life. Attempting to use intellect when instinct is warranted can result in the loss of life. Both have a valued role in achievement and survival. Intellect, and the ability to reason on a highly cognizant level, is what sets human life apart from all other life forms on earth.

18:10 The capability of being thoughtful has changed almost everything for humanity in the last 10,000 years. With new **circumstances, relationships,** and **potentials** constantly developing in society, thoughtfulness remains highly prized for adapting to change. Yet this process is not static nor does it remain current for long.

18:11 For the individual, routine review of beliefs held can result in a maturation of understanding. If done well this growth will take into account the endless changes witnessed in those around us, the structures we live within, and complexities of the ever-expanding possibilities of one's life. A respite may be sought from the effort needed to uphold this eternal unfoldment but the call for **thoughtful engagement** is quite often present.

18:12 When thoughtfulness is called for and instinct is returned a thoughtless reaction is issued in place of actions derived from greater consideration. How the actor deems this acceptable potentially routes the individual into similar behaviors leading in a life direction. This life direction is most likely not chosen, or understood by the actor as possessing **diminishing returns**. Here a thoughtless action leaves a mark upon the life of an individual that is unseen yet diverting from more purposeful interactions. This thoughtlessness can extend to every corner of one's life.

18:13 If efforts are given and focused upon, one will witness their willingness to advance their **situation, understanding,** and **appreciation for life**, seen and unseen. In these revelations one will come to understand there are no such real separate things as the haves and have nots; nor such real separate thing as **racism**, or **sexism**, or **ageism**. If one persist in using these terms to justify raw emotions one fails to accept that an overarching concept exist that addresses all of these vexations.

18:14 In our experience, if we are thoughtful, we choose the amount of love with which we respond to the world around us. This conceptual offering avails all who consider it a way to improve their station in this life. Friction in our experience is generated within the paradigm of: **"The Thoughtful and The Thoughtless."** As stated above this is intellect as opposed to instinct. Again, both have purpose. Yet both provide different services. Thoughtfulness is the grand unifier.

18:15 We need not agree with all propositions but accepting that others have their belief systems is intelligent. This is beyond instinct. Developing and engaging intellect delineates the challenges to overcome for many as they smooth their path. Thoughtfulness provides possibilities. If a single determination is needed between two or more divergent parties, solutions and reconciliations bring benefits.

18:16 Being thoughtful is not a call to be **acquiescent, pliant,** or **obedient**. It is a moment to develop a solution that is beneficial for all involved, or to appreciate that such a solution is unattainable. A forced solution is no solution. A peaceful resolution can be had by not entering into an agreement that is not beneficial. Thoughtfulness includes accepting what is. To move forward, what works for all must be appropriate. There is no failure in recognizing there are differences that must not be compromised. Being thoughtful is not **self-destructive, self-deceptive,** or necessarily **self-denying**.

18:17 A watchful eye must be kept to maintain **integrity-of-self**. Allowing one's self to be manipulated leads to being stifled, and to the Sinker mentality. The Sinker feels compelled to undermine and disable the Thinker because they are a perceived threat to the Sinker's desire for control. The Sinker is thoughtless to the potential of others. Thoughtless behavior disregards consequences. A person can act with love or lacking love but not in both fashions, from their perspective, at the same time. Thoughtfulness will compel the individual to respond with as much love as they are capable. Thoughtlessness, without regard, produces whatever comes out.

Chapter 19
How They Try to Kill
(Skimming the Surface)

19:01 Being respectful with someone
judgmental validates acceptance.

19:02 Someone judgmental can
become accepting by focusing
on real rights and responsibilities.

19:03 It is difficult for someone
judgmental to be honest.

19:04 Everyone is different.

19:05 Diversity makes
life worth living.

19:06 A person will never be
able to do everything in life.

19:07 The judgmental is set on
bringing everyone down to their
level of dissatisfaction.

19:08 People who dictate conditions
are oppressive and judgmental.

19:09 The goal of the oppressive
and judgmental is to dominate others.

19:10 The holding of one
political prisoner affects the
lives of countless others.

19:11 The oppressive and
judgmental uses one person
to get at others.

19:12 People are connected to
more people then they might suspect.

19:13 Every relationship a person
has connects them to even more people.

19:14 Beyond blood relations there
are people to whom we are connected.

19:15 People are connected to
people they do not even know.

19:16 Making one person sad can
lead to another person becoming sad.

19:17 The goal of the dictator
is to make everyone unhappy.

19:18 At the expense of the people,
luxuries are used to soothe the oppressor.

19:19 Unhappy people will
excuse oppressive people.

19:20 Oppression is
always unnecessary.

19:21 To relieve oppression
there must be freedom.

19:22 Some oppressive people
do not know they are oppressive.

19:23 Oppressive people use blame,
ridicule, and deceit to manipulate.

19:24 Manipulation can be
unconscious or intentional.

19:25 Hollow promises are bait for
manipulating the unaware and thoughtless.

19:26 Every lie accepted
leads closer to subjugation.

19:27 Subjugation removes individuality.

19:28 Removing individuality
from life is spiritual death.

19:29 Bold oppressors are hard to
resist; soft oppressors, nearly impossible.

19:30 Blaming others for one's failings
hastens one's downward trend.

19:31 Oppression and judgment are bent on creating lack.

19:32 Dehumanizing humanity is
the first step to its destruction.

19:33 An oppressor will do anything
to avoid examining their actions.

Chapter 19
How They Try to Kill
(Entering the Waters)

- Someone who wants to bring bodily, mental, or emotional harm to another ought not be dealt with in half measures.

- The deceit used by the oppressive to manipulate can be seen by the reasoning mind.

- The Sinker mindset needs to destroy anything that is contrary to its way.

- Once the Total Sinker begins to drag an individual or a population down they rarely stop on their own.

- To the Sinker, all must be rendered hopeless.

- Lack, dehumanizing humanity, and crushing individualism is the goal of the oppressive.

- Freedom is the only cure to oppression.

Chapter 19
How They Try to Kill
(Deeper Depths)

19:01 Being sensitive when dealing with Sinker behavior is the most **respectful** approach. This does not mean one should bend to its will. The Sinker mentality, by definition, is destructive. Why the Sinker does what they do is more often than not outside of their understanding. The mindset is motivational to the individual because of their insecurities and lack of a greater awareness of possibilities.

19:02 Yet even blinded by their motives the Sinker could mechanically take steps that would mitigate their behavior. Obviously, understanding the purpose of moderating their actions would be helpful, but understanding the concepts of **individual rights** and **responsibilities** is not so nebulous as to demand special training. To the Sinker, "live and let live," does not always apply and is more likely a one-sided proposition.

19:03 It is exceedingly difficult for the Total Sinker to honestly announce their motives. The emotions that dominate their life are ones of **rage, retribution,** and **hopelessness**. To change the world, whether at large or just in their circle, they speak words designed to motivate the unaware, placate the useful, and manipulate the thoughtless. This is all done while ridiculing those of opposing views. **Being untruthful is their modus operandi.** The Truth is unacceptable to those gripped by the Sinker mindset. As they set out to kill others they begin in small ways to kill themselves.

19:04 A goal of the Sinker mentality is to render all people equal. This is actually **undesirable, cruel,** and an **impossible fantasy**. There are no two identical people on this planet. Do not confuse equal rights under the law with making people equal. The combination of what motivates, enthralls, and pleases any one person cannot be found completely in any other person. We are all individuals.

19:05   The Total Sinker cannot embrace this concept. In their mind, the prospect of making all people equal is ideal, as it will make all things fair and everyone the same. This will never happen. Our diversity is one thing that makes life worth living. The sharing and partaking of new and interesting **perspectives, traditions,** and **experiences** bond us together while we open our hearts in love for our fellow human.

19:06   This does not mean we must engage in activities that do not appeal to us. There are too many possibilities available to engage them all. We pick and choose for ourselves. We do not close ourselves off to foreign offerings yet we trust our discernment to move us through this experience. The Sinker unrealistically makes **demands,** has useless **regulations,** and imposes strangulating **requirements.** This is the beginning to their killing process.

19:07   As in war, the objective of the Sinker mentality is to physically and/or spiritually kill those at odds with their belief system.

19:08   **Dictators** are a perfect example of the Sinker mindset. The dictator often comes to rule through violence of some kind. Ostensibly, they are there to change the status quo and to impose their idea of what is best for the people. To pacify the public a campaign is undertaken to quash the opposition, to put down the enthusiasm that opposes what the dictator stands for. This is done with class warfare and fantastical promises. Also the eradication of the opposition is pursued by ridiculing standards and morals, and with notions unrealized by the less-motivated and thoughtless.

19:09   The goal of the dictator is to physically and spiritually dominate the population. A country would not work if there were no population. To get the bulk of the population in line they are **brutalized** into a state of spiritual lack. Taxation and deprivation along with the restriction of movement, worship, and expression are some of the tools used to dominate the population. Those who do not succumb must be **murdered, driven away,** or **imprisoned.**

19:10 When the Sinker regime takes a single political prisoner the lives of countless others are affected. The prisoner could be a middle-aged man. This person is a grandson, a grandnephew, a son, a nephew, a husband, a brother, a cousin, a father, an uncle, a grandfather, a great uncle, and an in-law, informal and otherwise.

19:11 By imprisoning this one person the dictator has effected the lives of so many. Attacking the loving hearts of the relatives by the imprisonment and ill-treatment of this one person diminishes the spirits of a vast group. Let us elaborate upon this premise.

19:12 We will start with a hypothetical prisoner; a man in his late 40s. Looking only at he and his father's side of the family he is a grandfather and his grandparent's, siblings and descendants are all still living. For this example we will posit a **0 percent population growth**. This person is a grandson **(to two)**, a grand nephew **(to two)**, a son **(to two)**, a nephew **(to two)**, a first cousin, one-time removed **(to six)**, a husband **(to one)**, a brother **(to one)**, a first cousin **(to two)**, a second cousin **(to four)**, a father **(to two)**, an uncle **(to two)**, a second cousin, one-time removed **(to eight)**, a grandfather **(to four)**, a great uncle **(to four)**, a first cousin, two-times removed **(to eight)**, a second cousin, two-times removed **(to sixteen)**, and an in-law **(to twenty-five, informal and otherwise)**.

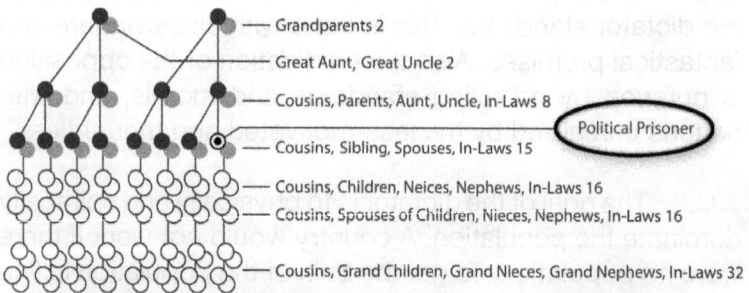

— Grandparents 2
— Great Aunt, Great Uncle 2
— Cousins, Parents, Aunt, Uncle, In-Laws 8
Political Prisoner
— Cousins, Sibling, Spouses, In-Laws 15
— Cousins, Children, Neices, Nephews, In-Laws 16
— Cousins, Spouses of Children, Nieces, Nephews, In-Laws 16
— Cousins, Grand Children, Grand Nieces, Grand Nephews, In-Laws 32

19:13 If the prisoner's grandfather had only one sibling and every offspring thereafter only had one sibling, and each only two offspring (to establish 0 percent population growth), the total number of people effected over five generations is **91,** not counting the prisoner. But those 91 people are only on the prisoner's immediate side of his father's family. Add in the **grandmothers'** side of the family **(2 sets),** the missing **mothers', aunts', uncles',** and **cousins'** sides of the family **(4 sets),** and the missing **wives', husbands',** and **cousins'** families **(24 sets),** and the number expands to over **2,000.** Granted, this may be a complex and confusing calculation but it well illustrates the structure of interdependent loving hearts that is the core of the family. This is primarily why Totalitarianism, and related ideologies, along with the Sinker mentality first seek to dissolve the family.

19:14 These may not all be blood relations but they are associations, informal and otherwise - if not by marriage still close enough that they might be thoughtfully invited to a family gathering. In the graphical accounting on the previous page not all cousins are included. Also not included are the families of the grandparents, parents, cousins, and spouses among the second tier of relations found in the missing families of the first tier grandmothers/grandfathers, mothers/fathers, aunts/uncles, wives/husbands, and cousins.

19:15 Additionally, there is no accounting for friends and strangers who learn of the imprisonment. This is all predicated on 0 percent population growth. The numbers expand exponentially when the number of offspring is increased. The point is: murdering, driving away, or imprisoning one individual has the potential to impact a huge number of otherwise **innocent relations.**

19:16 The sadness felt by each of these people is felt by those around them and spreads like a virus through the community. It may not be discernible on the surface yet it is there. One less smile has a domino **effect that cascades** through the population. This is the goal of the dictator. This is the goal of the Total Sinker.

19:17 The survivors will need to continue their lives and produce something on which to subsist. With the emotional burden of the imprisoned family member this becomes an additional hardship. The dictator counts on this as they suppress the population in an attempt to lower their spirit in line with that of the dictator and the **Sinker mentality**.

19:18 Quite often the dictator will surround themselves with the luxuries the common people cannot afford for themselves. Through taxation they will do this at the expense of the population. This is how they attempt to soothe their **rage-filled, egocentric, and hopeless heart**.

19:19 The ally to the dictator will speak of the tyrant's rule as being necessary for national success. The supporter will go further to laud the dictator as being, "of the people," and a, "national hero," and in **tortured logic** ridicule the dictator's detractors.

19:20 Trampling the liberties of individuals is nothing short of **tyranny**. Tyranny is always unnecessary. Support of a tyrant is a ruse and reveals the Sinker mentality of the supporter, as all wait, with an eye to the horizon, for the promised success. Decades later success is still being waited for, the dictator still lives in luxury, and the objects of ridicule are the same successful and freedom loving individuals and nations.

19:21 The population has been suppressed, and while abandoning their soul, the dictator has achieved their goal. This is their thoughtless aim. To counter this predicament, thoughtful **reason** must be applied.

19:22 Away from the dictatorial oppression that so much of the population of earth has and has to endure, others are working to **mislead, manipulate,** and **control**. Many are unaware of how damaging their efforts are.

19:23 The Sinker tools used to garner political, community, and commercial support include the **blaming** and **ridiculing** of others. This method is age old. The techniques have been vaunted as a cure-all for the struggling would-be leader. As always these efforts are cloaked in doing the people's work.

19:24   While some efforts are honest, yet misdirected, many are bold attempts to subjugate whole populations. Whether **nationally, community-wide,** or **ethnically** these usurpers of human dignity are focused and prey upon the weakest of spirit in the population. These downcast individuals are the prime targets for the Sinker.

19:25   Hollow promises are the bait used to entice the **unaware** and **thoughtless**. The largess, which these so-called leaders dangle before their prey is never a product of their own efforts. Always the support they buy is with other people's money. The promise of something for nothing is too grand of an opportunity to resist for the oppressed and those already put upon by the Sinker mentality.

19:26   With every lie swallowed the prey steps closer to the chute that will take them downward to the utter destruction of their **will, expression,** and **individuality**. Each step deploys a deeper-rooted connection of reciprocation that will be expected by the Sinker system. The prey will come to accept this reciprocation as they are incrementally converted to the mindset.

19:27   In this conversion the Sinker initiate will be stripped of their individuality and added to the heaps of followers. Spoken to as belonging with special groups these followers will be drenched in patronizing language crafted to obscure their fate. This is designed to **depersonalize** them, rendering them divorced from, and nearly incapable of, the desires in their loving heart.

19:28   This is a process to **spiritually kill** the initiate and leave them hopeless. There is nothing uplifting about not being who and what you are in your loving heart. Submitting to the group identity will become paramount. There is no inspiration available when one lives at the patronage of someone else. All will hinge on being a good follower.

19:29   This will close around the initiate until they are locked in place and wholly without the knowledge of their personal ability to extricate themselves. In the presence of a bold tyrant this will be hard to resist and when promulgated under **soft tyranny**, almost impossible to resist.

19:30 The perceived benefits gained by accusations of fault aimed at others for one's own shortcomings grooves a **slippery slope downward**. The thoughtless spewing of venomous rebukes accumulates as tiny weights pulling the spirit down. The handler guiding the hapless soul into a dark place of hopelessness encourages all this. **This is how they kill.**

19:31 **Emotionally, physically,** and **spiritually** the Sinker mentality draws the ill-informed to a state of lack. The Sinker mindset seeks to neutralize and degrade all situations so as to draw everything into the lower frequencies that mark its experience.

19:32 In **dehumanizing** the population the sanctity of human life is crushed. The individual is thought of as unimportant. This is because the human spirit is an anathema to the Sinker mentality. This is because the human spirit is inspired to rise out of the control of the Sinker, leaving the Sinker to its natural state, fully revealing its mindset of **remorse, hopelessness,** and **humiliation**.

19:33 The Sinker only wants to keep their head above the water and will do anything to forestall their downward trend. This includes sacrificing others to the fate they are directing themselves to assume. **This is why they try to kill.**

Chapter 20
The Power To Love
(Skimming the Surface)

20:01 Love can create an
uplifting condition in one's life.

20:02 Love does not judge.

20:03 Life is about how we
act and react to the things
we encounter everyday.

20:04 We can act and react
to the world around us
through our instincts.

20:05 We can act and react to
the world around us using our intellect.

20:06 Our instincts and intellect
are revealed in our actions.

20:07 Our actions will reflect one
of three attitudes, love, hate, and neutrality.

20:08 Hate is actually a lack of love.

20:09 Everything we do can be
measured on a scale of love.

20:10 What we create
will be returned to us.

20:11 How we act will be
reflected in our surroundings.

20:12 A person might become like,
or be repulsed by, what they encounter.

20:13 A person might change to
match an influence or be driven away.

20:14 A person can influence
something to match them.

20:15 Two people who do not
match might not be influenced to match.

20:16 Everyone can choose
love and in so, influence those they
might, to match that love.

20:17 There is no way to truly
understand why one does not choose love.

20:18 A person chooses if they will love.

20:19 A person can possibly
influence someone else
to match their actions.

20:20 A person may repulse, or be
repulsed by, something or someone else.

20:21 A person may change
to match the influence of
something or someone else.

20:22 Everyone has an influential
feeling they express which can
be called their, "essence."

20:23 Everyone's essence will
match a recognizable rate of,
"vibrational frequency."

20:24 Everyone has a most-loving
and a least-loving self.

20:25 Physical harm, murder,
suicide, and emotional abuse
are counterproductive.

20:26 Every person decides for
themselves what anything means to them.

20:27 Actions without thought are instinctive.

20:28 Actions with thought are intellectual.

20:29 All actions will attract similar
thoughts and actions through spiritual gravity.

20:30 All actions possess
spiritual mass, mass equals
gravity, gravity attracts.

20:31 There is love in every situation.

20:32 People are the channels
through which universal
love is made manifest.

20:33 Universal love is made
manifest through thoughts and actions.

20:34 The spoken word
delivers influential energy.

20:35 The expansion of our experience
is limitless when we choose love.

Chapter 20
The Power To Love
(Entering the Waters)

- Love is of supreme benefit to body, mind, and spirit.

- As a way of life, we can choose love.

- When we act we show favor, disfavor, and neutrality.

- How we act toward ourselves and the world is reflected back to us.

- All people, things, and situations pull and/or push upon us in an attempt to influence us. We at the same time are pulling and/or pushing upon every person, thing, and situation we encounter presenting our influence.

- Every person is pulled upon to become more like what they encounter, the encountered can be pulled to become more like the person, or, one or both sides push apart from the other. This pulling and/or pushing is always happening.

Chapter 20
The Power To Love
(Deeper Depths)

What Is The Power To Love?

20:01 **The Power To Love** is the ability to center one's life in an uplifting condition. Because no two people understand, believe, or live in the same way, the individual best discerns improvement in this matter. With The Power To Love it is possible to alter our surroundings and inspire those near us to create their own uplifting condition. The mechanics for this process are elementary and easily attained with **confidence, discipline,** and **consistency**.

20:02 The process is to love **ceaselessly** and to reflect with **great appreciation, gratitude,** and **joy** upon the uplifting physical and emotional events of one's life, present or desired. Importantly, this is done while trusting one's intuition with impersonal **neutrality**, and remaining free of judgment of one's self, others, and the world around us.

20:03 In our lives we respond to myriad demands placed upon us daily. Endlessly, we are confronted with **people, situations,** and **events** that call for our reaction. This is the foundation of life. Countless times everyday moments appear in which we must decide what we are going to do in regards to something someone said, how circumstances we encounter and plans we have evolve, or an action that might or has taken place. Our response is a representation of us, at that moment, and comes from one of two sources within our being.

20:04 A response could first spring from our **instinctual self** - a source of unconscious determination that for millennia has protected humankind. Instinct still serves us greatly occasionally in life-or-death situations but often it also overshadows our lives with unnecessary displays of egocentric behavior and desires.

20:05   The other source of response to daily life can issue from our **intellectual self**, what many recognize as our **mind**. This more recently developed source of conscious action is predicated on the reasoning we possess or have developed for ourselves. This reasoning encompasses our belief system in regards to the **unconditional love** we have for humanity, **truth** as we see it, **wisdom** we recognize from within ourselves along with our connection to the world and things greater than ourselves.

20:06   Both sources undergo changes throughout our lives. Our instincts are largely inborn yet are conditioned as we unconsciously experience our world. Our intellect, while partly inborn, is greatly a conscious outgrowth of our thoughts and ruminations on our life experience. Both sources provide us with motivations as we are called upon to act in this world. The response we choose or the emotions we allow to motivate us come from within us and are ours to control. Ultimately, what we do in this life is our responsibility. How we act shows our self to the world.

20:07   The power we have at our command and the choices we make in responding to people, situations, and events reveals us, at that moment, to be centered in one of three dispositions. These three dispositions are: **"I love it,"** **"I hate it,"** or, **"whatever."** Generally speaking, these are the three, "flavors," our actions will reinforce. Respectively, one is more positive, one, to a large degree, is less positive, and one is neutral. Each can be placed on a scale denoting quantity of the single element at the heart of all matter and emotion. That element is **love**.

20:08   There is no such thing as hatred. Just like there is no such thing as a source of darkness. Darkness is the lack or absence of light. Actions that are equated with hate are simply actions that lack love, as we perceive the positive nature of love. This is important because

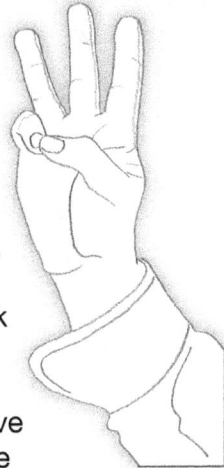

every action contains some level and directed focus of what we call love. The intensity and focus of that love is what manifest in an action.

20:09 The intensity of love in any action matches a point on the scale of, **"positivity,"** as we understand it. Much like the presence or absence of light in a physical setting, this scale represents the gradation of love in all actions. As we act we determine, either by **instinct** or **intellect**, the amount of love in our actions, whether by ability or will. The importance of this is found in the disposition we choose to center ourselves in as we engage The Power To Love.

20:10 One would find this to be important because what we create with our actions we receive back as reinforced actions, both our own and of those around us. This colors our world. A less-positive action will often motivate someone to instinctively return a response in kind. An intellectual response to a less-positive action takes more effort and thought and is more likely to be more-positive if not simply neutral. The neutral disposition can be a developed response created to disengage any further interaction with the confronting person, situation, or event.

20:11 A continually supported disposition will permeate people, situations, and events in one's surroundings. Which means one's surroundings will come to reflect the disposition one supports ranging from, "more-positive," to, "less-positive."

20:12 Alternate to this, because conscious participants are free to choose which disposition they will support, people, situations, and events may change due to repulsion of or attraction to a disparate disposition. The only remaining option is a person may consciously or unconsciously convert to the disposition supported by people, situations, and events that surround them. These dispositions can be thought of as **vibrational frequencies** that are either harmonious or discordant.

20:13 Any interaction will result in two main alternate

outcomes. First, between two parties, if they do not already match, one will **assume** the vibrational frequency of the other, either by raising or lowering the disposition they support, becoming either more-positive or less-positive, whichever is more dominate and accepted. Secondly, the vibrational frequencies are **sufficiently discordant** that one or both parties separates from interaction.

20:14 More succinctly, a person becomes, or already matches, what they are exposed to. Or what a person is exposed to mirrors them. Or finally, there is a split between the parties as one or both determines the other to be undesirable. In the case that one is inanimate it is simply avoided having been found undesirable by the conscious animated participant.

20:15 There is one last scenario that can occur. A conscious animated participant can encounter a discordant vibrational frequency and, while being at odds with the newly encountered frequency, may wish to **empathize** with and influence it. If the second party is capable of change and resist, not wishing to assume the disposition of the first, some change must be made by or in the first party to create harmony. This assumes the first party is willing and/or capable of change. If over time the change does not occur a split will most likely take place even if a conscious desire to empathize still exist. To truly empathize a conscious and **vibrational equivalence** needs to be achieved.

20:16 Every thinking, feeling, human being has within them The Power To Love and in that power the ability to center their life experience in a condition of their choosing, most powerfully if they **consciously decide** to choose.

20:17 Intellectually, most desire love while instinctively many pursue dominance from within less-positive dispositions through misguided egocentric behaviors. The unrecognized ability or unwillingness to engage The Power To Love portends unknown realities within the individual. **Awareness Through Reflection** is the prescription by which individuals can discover their own potential.

20:18 Only the individual can uncover their ability and only they can engage their willingness to exercise The Power To Love. When we do this we benefit ourselves, and the world at large, **today** and into the **future**.

These Are The Options

20:19 **1.** Your surroundings, events, or the people with whom you interact match, or come to more closely reflect, your essence. (By your thoughts and behavior you match or influence the environment, activities, and people near you, to experience and support a change in a related vibrational frequency that comes to harmonize with your vibration.)

20:20 **2.** You repulse, or are repulsed by, the essence of objects, events, surroundings, or someone you come into contact with. (A presence, yours or one you encounter, is either more-positive, less-positive, or somehow unrecognizably different and it is determined by one or both parties to be undesirable, creating a split between the parties.)

20:21 **3.** You come to reflect the essence of objects, events, surroundings, or persons with whom you interact. (Due to the dominant or accepted presence of things, activities, localities, or persons near you, consciously or unconsciously, your vibrational frequency raises or lowers to harmonize with that presence.)

Components of The Power To Love

20:22 **"Essence,"** is a word used to denote the vibrational frequency of a person, situation, object, or event. This is related to a scale of more positive to less positive, as it is widely accepted matching proportionately and respectively to love and the lack of love as we each understand love.

20:23 **"Vibrational Frequency,"** is a term used to describe the rate and amplitude of an emotional or spiritual property which is emitted, sensed or not, from all matter animate and inanimate.

20:24 Within every person is a gamut of instinct and intellect that encompasses their most-loving self and their least-loving self. From which portion of that scale we act is our choice. As we act we will likely gravitate to a centralized disposition that will in time characterize our general personality. This disposition matches our essence.

20:25 **Personally counterproductive actions are;** inflicting physical harm to the human body, including murder and suicide, and the exacerbation of the emotional state of the innocent and the weak, this can include ourselves. In the opinion of many, other actions may be thought of as counterproductive yet are potentially more injurious to the perpetrator than the intended victim.

20:26 What someone does cannot matter to someone else until the second party **responds** to the original act.

20:27 If the response is made by default, and instinctual, then the response is made without intellectual engagement. This source of response is potentially appropriate and beneficial yet may more likely reflect a **thoughtless herd mentality** action inbred with base survival instincts.

20:28 If the response is made using intellect, thought, regardless of foundation, has been engaged. Reviewing currently held belief systems affords the individual their best opportunity to have the most well founded intellect upon which to draw appropriate responses.

20:29 How one chooses to pursue this existence can be an ever-evolving experience offering many opportunities for expansion. Some choices will return a more mundane reality, stocked with the default actions of an unengaged intellect. As sure as gravity attracts mass, more-positive and less-positive actions will render commensurate fruit.

20:30 All actions possess the essence of **spiritual mass**. Over time, love returns love, and actions that lack love, return actions that lack love. Through this we ask for our experience by our actions.

How The Power To Love Works

20:31 **The Power To Love** works by seeing the positive in any situation; by seeing beyond fearfully misidentified markers of shortcomings; by viewing without judgment what the ego objects to in any setting; by trusting that in all circumstances purpose and providence inhabit the people, surroundings, and events of one's life.

20:32 Love is not created by humankind yet is manifest in this world through humankind. We are the conduits of the **Infinite Love** of . . . (fill in the blank), call it what you will. **The Single Source** of our creation does not have a qualm as to what we name it. Power has been deposited in certain forms of interaction which include; names, words, and activities, yet a connection made between an intelligent life form and the higher level of consciousness that is the stem of our existence is possible through personally defined methods as well. A voice directed at the origin of our experience is always heard. And the hearing of a **Divine** response resonates within our hearts.

20:33 The heart is the channel through which love enters the physical universe. From there our thoughts and actions manifest its conveyance. By becoming, within our abilities and willingness, this channel of love, we **harmonize** with higher levels of love and draw into our life the uplifting benefits. Focused thought upon the most desirable of circumstances strengthens our emotional and intellectual bonds with the **Infinite.**

20:34 The spoken word delivers influential energy. Speak of what you love. Forgo speaking of what you, **"hate."** Build what you love and what stood in your way will be replaced. To tear down with hate leaves little in place including in the heart that used hate as a force.

20:35 The expansion of our experience is limitless when, to the greatest of our abilities, we open our heart and engage **The Power To Love**.

Your 3 Choices

"Whatever"

"I Love It"

"I Hate It"

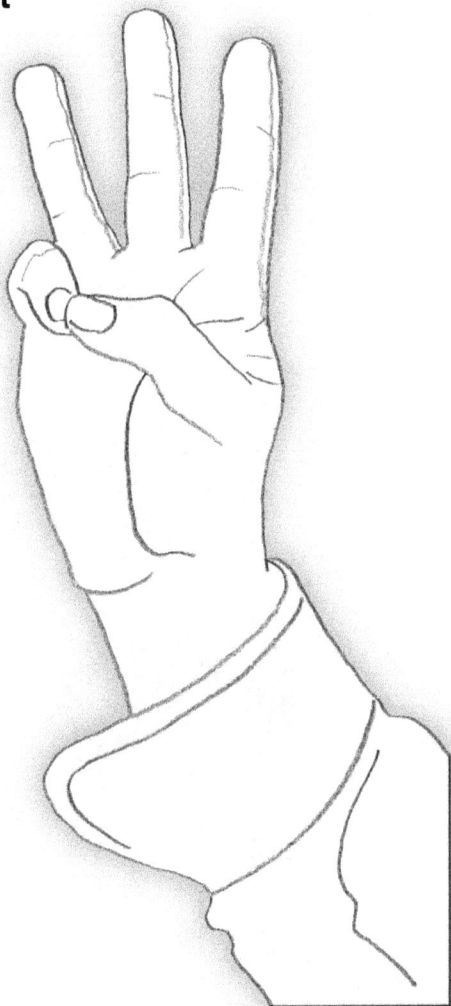

Know your choices and what they produce.

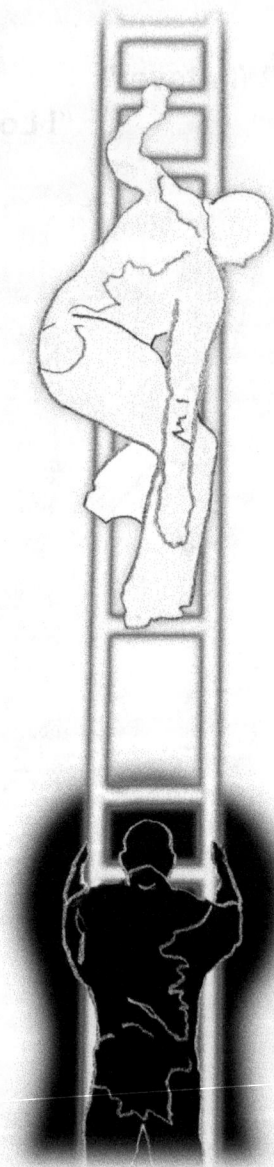

Knowing of **morality** and not living morally reveals an inability or an unwillingness. Both do not prove morality as meaningless only that, for the actor, it is unattained.

The Sinker likely knows of their connection to the uplifting **supernatural** essence yet is unable or unwilling to bask in its inspiration. This does not prove it worthless only not accessed. Where we go is at our direction.

The rights of the individual are immutable and while understood by **history** they have been contorted into a new meaning in line with the corrupting mindset of the Sinker.

Words used to express the **sovereignty** of men, referring to all individually, have been changed to corral humankind into the rights of man, referring to all collectively. This was the beginning of separating people from their new found **liberties**.

Human nature portents our heroic race, its feet of clay, and **Divinity** unclaimed. We make ourselves more whole when we freely give to each other.

Chapter 21

Awareness
(Skimming the Surface)

21:01 A person is not born a blank slate.

21:02 Friction can occur when things
or ideas rub against each other.

21:03 Attitude is one's self-accepted way of
thinking, and a relationship in movement.

21:04 Perspective is a way someone
thinks about or looks at something.

21:05 Living life we travel through time/space.

21:06 Through reason, long ago humankind came to
recognize our Creative Source.

21:07 Logically, every person was
created with a life purpose.

21:08 If a person follows their heart they
will be led to their life purpose.

21:09 There is no way to escape
the Source of our creation.

21:10 The Source of our creation is
mostly beyond human understanding.

21:11 It is meaningless that we would be
created only to be destroyed after this life.

21:12 Humans have changed plants
and animals for human purposes.

21:13 Humans can largely change
their lives to suit their desire.

21:14 To change one's life, deep
understanding of life is beneficial.

21:15 Life is more than
objects and movement.

21:16 The way a person acts can
influence others to act.

21:17 Happiness seeks to create happiness -
sadness seeks to create sadness.

21:18 The circumstance into which
a person is born is merely a starting point.

21:19 How a life is led is
up to the individual.

21:20 How we think and look at
life will lead us to our conclusions.

21:21 At all times all matter is
changing yet mostly appears unchanging.

21:22 Everything we do we think of as
the most desirable thing to do at the time.

21:23 Life is what one makes of it, so it cannot be unfair.

21:24 Understanding one's own
level of consciousness is of great value.

21:25 Humility is the path to uncover
less-desirable traits in one's self.

21:26 To the friction of the physical
universe, love is the ultimate lubricant.

21:27 Inspiring one's self to achieve
is the greatest goal, leading to all others.

21:28 Recognizing one's own
shortcomings is a challenge.

21:29 The primitive part of the
human brain is the source of
primitive behavior.

21:30 An extreme reaction to life
is often of primitive behavior.

21:31 Ridicule is a base response
of primitive behavior.

21:32 Ridicule strikes directly
at the primitive brain.

21:33 Running from truth is a
primitive response.

21:34 If one dwells in their primitive brain
it is difficult to gain perspective of the self.

21:35 The complex part of the
human brain controls speech and reason.

21:36 What a person thinks
reveals if they more use their
complex brain or primitive brain.

21:37 Gaining perspective on one's
level of awareness is a worthy endeavor.

21:38 A person can be uplifting
simply by being loving and accepting.

21:39 If a person builds something with
love they focus on being a loving person.

Chapter 21

Awareness
(Entering the Waters)

- What gives a person the awareness they have for any situation is a combination of many attributes.

- How we gain and develop personal and situational awareness is a unique formula to every individual.

- Having awareness of one's self, life, and surroundings, among other factors, creates an experience.

- Without deep reflection all things are beyond greater understanding.

- Every moment is a point from which to move forward.

- Whether with humility or ridicule we reveal our self and our awareness in our actions.

Chapter 21

Awareness
(Deeper Depths)

21:01 We start our life with a **perspective, character,** and **personality** handed down to us from our ancestors. With our input, the environment we enter into influences the cultivation of the direction of our life path. As we grow and learn we further develop ourselves by where we go, what we see, and how we choose to respond to that experience. This is why we ought to **explore, reflect upon,** and **refine** the matters of our lives. The uniqueness that is our life is a reflection of the uniqueness of our experience combined with our own unique being.

21:02 Only one **person, animal,** or **object** can occupy any given location in the physical universe at a time. When two things come into contact there is a potential for friction. The word friction comes from the Latin, **"fricare,"** meaning to rub. Friction creates resistance and resistance creates friction. Ideas can rub upon the mind of a person. Ideas can cause friction. Thoughts can create friction in the mind. Yet this mental friction mostly comes into play when events are perceived, thoughts are conceived, and actions are taken.

21:03 It is said, **"attitude is everything."** If considered, one might agree that intellectually, perspective comes before an intense and focused attitude. Without forethought a person simply reacts by instinct. The word attitude comes from the Latin, **"aptus,"** meaning **fit**. An attitude is a settled upon or fit and accepted way of thinking. Another definition of attitude regards positioning, which can equate to angle, as in a direction one is oriented toward, relative to the direction in which they are moving.

21:04 The angle from which a person looks at something is called their **perspective**. A vantage point is a perspective either mental or physical. One first observes from an angle (perspective), then acts from an angle (attitude), and finally, if the individual is aware they will consider the events that had occurred and with sufficient reflection, add to their understanding of their world as they continue their life heading off on their unique path in a unique direction. As it happens this unique direction can be equated with another angle. If perspective informs attitude then more specifically, **"perspective is everything."**

21:05 Where we are, what we do, and where we go is all part of the linear experience we know as **time/space**. Living life we travel through time/space. The before, during, and after portion of each experience has everything to do with the angles we either view from, act toward, or pursue after an event. Our choice is the final factor that determines these angles. Everything is **perspective, attitude,** and the resulting **direction**, chosen or not, in that order. This is the three-dimensional universe of time/space.

21:06 The conditions we inhabit are defined by our ability to **conceive** and **perceive** the parameters and matter of our environment. The understanding gathered through reflection and reason long ago led to deduce a **Creative Source** responsible for our origin. This **Uplifting Supernatural Essence** has been given many names. The word, **"GOD,"** is the same as the Anglo-Saxon word for, **"supreme good."** Regardless of the name, to the witness all representations are of the same essence. Titles and mythologies attributed to this Supernatural Essence reflect the concepts and language used by this **Infinite Intelligence** to communicate with the respective parties.

21:07 In our coming into being it is reasonable to conjecture we are prepared by this Creative Source to enter into a situation in line with a purpose. There is no logic in not having a purpose. And if GOD is anything it is logical. There are those who will dispute the concept of an individual having a specific life mission. Some may wish to argue this concept as it applies to them but to do so regarding another does not show forethought. To do so would illustrate a lack of understanding for the totality and appreciation another person has for their life.

21:08 A person need not know their life mission to fulfill it. The surest way to discover and/or fulfill a life mission is through an open heart. This facilitates the willingness and ability to manifest love. People who have a hard time with this logic usually struggle with the concepts of a Creative Source and life after death. Both are forgone conclusions if life is to have any meaning whatsoever.

21:09 **A Divine Consciousness** that is all-powerful, all-knowing, and all-present is inescapable. We are inextricably a part of this Supernatural Essence and are in a sense sent forth from it. Part of the proof for this is our ability to reason. The enlightenment that humankind arrived upon was our Divine making. In other words we were made, whole or otherwise, by our ascent into our reasoning mind. In possessing a reasoning mind we obtain influence over the process of living life.

21:10 Whatever one calls this essence the concept of an **Infinite Consciousness** immediately burst beyond any reasonable person's ability to fully comprehend. If a person accepts the concept of the **Creative Source** all they have is their understanding of it. A person can believe in something without knowing fully what it is. Though maybe not well founded the belief can be somewhat correctly formed. But a person cannot disbelieve in something if they do not know what it is. They merely disbelieve in what they think it is. With the infinite of possibilities posited in the concept of GOD, a person is left to accept the concept of something greater than the self or disbelieve in the finite conception of what they think it is.

21:11 It is unfathomable for the **Infinite Divine Consciousness** to allow the spark of reason found in humankind to exist and to extinguish that spark, and the consciousness attached to it, at the end of our corporeal existence. What is more widely understood is that we share in this spark as it is, and as are we, a part of the **Divine Mind** that created this experience. And in this life we have our unique journey, which then, as implausible as this may seem, can inform and express the **Infinite**.

21:12 The **instinctual script** that dominates the life of plants and animals is unavailable to those species for alteration. Plants and animals do not possess the necessary intellect to change their existence. The script or software program running as that plant and animal is largely set. In these programs there is the slightest available space for gradual evolutionary changes. These changes are unconsciously engaged in the plant or animal. This is quite natural and normal. Through domestication humans have altered the software of plants and animals. But this is done to the human's desire and again is not available to the altered species.

21:13 Humans are **self-editing software** running a program designed to render unique results. We do this to a heightened degree regardless of how we engage life. This is because we can thoughtfully and emotionally respond to the **objects, events, persons,** and **situations** of life. Yet being self-editing does not assure editing will be pursued.

21:14 What this software represents is simply a blueprint for future action. Contemplating this concept takes more than a reaction from the reptilian, or primitive center of the human brain. Witness how you feel about that concept. Consider deeply the possibility that we live lives with purpose and reason and that as it is presently set we are moving along a pre-determined, yet editable path. How we engage our purpose and with what form of reasoning is up to us. This is why a **spiritualist** will implore the living of a life considering the unseen.

21:15 The **illusion** of fractured light is fleeting. Perspective determines everything. Light sources come and go. With reason one can imagine. Imagination is the key to unlock doors of perception and ignorance. The imagination can build a bridge between the known and the yet to be known using **intellect, reason,** and **introspection**.

21:16 This process leads us to edit our experience, to redraw our **blueprint for future action.** This behavior can influence and inspire others to do the same. This is partly why we tell stories. When humanity was less-aware mythology was created to guide our self-editing process.

21:17 Everything has some potential influence, consciously intended or not. This can guide the self-editing process within human awareness. This illuminates the interaction between the two mindsets found in humankind. First there is the **Thinker mindset** that seeks expansion and the inevitable rise in awareness of self and concepts greater than the self. And then there is the **Sinker mindset** that is constrictive and hopeless, and bent on drawing humanity back into a primordial shell of confusion and limited self-awareness. Those of the Sinker mindset, while unable or unwilling to love, hope to soothe their feelings of insecurity by judging others and denying reality.

21:18 The script or software we enter into this life with is but a starting point. These programs are not **static, routine,** or **duplicates**. The self-editing software programs running as every individual life are **dynamic, unusual,** and **unique**. This is something the Total Sinker cannot begin to comprehend.

21:19 How we edit our software is up to us. We either use our intellect, however developed, or we rest on our instinct and allow this world, life, and ourselves to be unexplored - emitting base behaviors in response to our experience. The choice is between being **thoughtful** and **thoughtless**.

21:20 What and how we think of life will direct us to our conclusions. Whether in a Thinker manner rising to challenges or in a Sinker way blaming and gnashing our teeth, we select our path. The ancient and highly regarded **Greek philosopher Heraclitus** (born circa 535 B.C., died circa 475 B.C.), spent his life focused on this question. The flux with which one can address any object, situation, event, or person changes every second. He wrote, **"Everything changes and nothing remains still."**

21:21 To crystallize this thought Heraclitus proposed that life was like a flowing river and as one steps into the river they can never step into it again in the same way because the water, and time, moves pass. In his work he resolved there is a forming and dissolving of all things constantly cycling before us. On a sub-atomic level this is theoretically presumed. The **Hindu** god **Shiva's Tandava** is a dance representing the source of the cycle of **creation, preservation,** and **dissolution.** Heraclitus named this balanced state of building up and tearing down, **"Strife."** We do not see this change yet it is constant. But to our eye the objects, situations, events, and people of our life seem fairly set. Heraclitus named this balanced state of our observation, **"Justice."**

21:22 Everything can be looked at from more than one angle. When we decide which angle we will view something, we pronounce our perspective to be . . . **"Just."** Yet in the ever-changeable possibilities in things we do not control, or things we are unhappy with, we find, **"Strife."** Heraclitus also wrote, " . . . **strife is justice** . . . " As in the physical universe it is so true for the mental universe, anything can change and what we decide to do we confirm as being the most desirable at that moment.

21:23 Some think strife, and also life, is unfair. Yet we know life is what we make of it. So if it is something that one makes for themselves it cannot be unfair. Life is **made, perceived,** and **adjusted** by our own hand and mind. Only the Sinker would see their creation and efforts as unfair. The ultimate nature of life is fairness because we decide how we will regard life. This shows the separation between the Thinker and the Sinker. In polarity the two mindsets are connected but different. It is not so much that they are on the same scale of consciousness as much as they are at different places on that shared scale. In this, one can go from one mindset to the other by changing their thoughts and actions. Unmistakably this goes in both directions.

21:24 Personally coming to some understanding of where we as individuals are on the scale of conscious awareness serves our best interest. Reflecting upon our thoughts and behaviors will aid us in reading, and redrawing, as desired, the blueprint of our future life and actions. This is the gift given humankind in our creation in the Divine image. Pursuing this goal possess a distinct set of challenges.

21:25   A person moving through a medium of consciousness will find it difficult to evidence the conditions that for their life have been invisible. How one can identify less-desirable traits in themselves is a performance of humility. Admitting to one's own shortcomings is a bold step forward. Altering one's life trajectory in the hopes of producing uplifting effects, one may risk; relationships, shelter, and sustenance. If these efforts are truly uplifting they stand to produce self-acceptance and a willingness toward greater things. This path forward and upward is found in **The Power To Love**.

21:26   To the friction of the physical universe love is the ultimate lubricant, smoothing all movement. Recognizing that the resistance in judgment is countered by the acceptance in love reveals this fact. For one to know how much of a Sinker they are can be difficult. Whether growing up in a condition or incrementally being transformed into it, accepting why one lives in **anger, vanity, arrogance,** or **hate** is sometimes hard. It is one thing to be controlled by these emotions and another to see oneself without bias. This cathartic epiphany comes from the surrender to something greater than the self. However that manifest. It comes from the heart and results in greater awareness. Awareness makes things possible through **acceptance** and **willingness**.

21:27   Achieving an elevated status among humanity is not the goal. Inspiring one, even if it is oneself, is the same as inspiring many. Being who and what we are as individuals, within our understanding of life and uplifting thoughts and actions, is the best that we can obtain. Measuring oneself by the standards of others will not produce the purest outcome. A lifetime of reflection upon what is most desirable will refine one into the fullest Thinker possible. One does not gain awareness of themselves by living someone else's life. We are who we are from the inside out. Searching for self worth outside of ourselves will not produce genuine results. The awareness of the loving individual we have been created to be will stem from, and forever be reinforced in, our heart.

21:28 Knowing that the Sinker exists gives us signs to be wary of. Recognizing the Sinker within is an arduous undertaking. The Thinker does not seek to call themselves **angry, deceitful,** or **grim**. The Sinker cannot appreciate that they are **lacking love**. The Thinker knows that love is always the reason for life. It is onerous for the Sinker to concede they feel unwilling, incapable, or feel unworthy of love. Confessing to the burdensome, calls out the Sinker mindset. This divulgence exposes the behavior for revision. Until a life situation is accepted, conditions that perpetuate the Sinker mentality cannot be explored.

21:29 The **R-Complex**, the **primitive**, or the **reptilian brain**, is the portion of the human brain that drives the Sinker mentality. This corresponds, in part, with the root chakra and other energy centers lower in the body. The fight-or-flight response is attributed to the primitive brain. This survival technique is activated without conscious consideration of circumstances.

21:30 **Fight-or-flight** is often a quick and extreme reaction to **people, events, situations, objects,** and **ideas**. The first reaction will be to subdue the offending matter in whatever way possible. This is the fight response. The alternate reaction will be to run away from the situation. That is the flight response. The fight-or-flight response can be stress related. Both are out of self-preservation, whether warranted or not.

21:31 Fight-or-flight is activated to disengage from whatever it was that triggered the response. If one tries to kill an aggressor or simply run away from it, the idea is to eliminate the interaction. Without physically murdering the opposition the fight response can be engaged to **devalue, diminish,** or **dehumanize** the opposition to render it unable to be persuasive. To render opposition impotent, a base behavior is often employed . . . **ridicule**.

21:32 Ridicule strikes directly at the primitive brain. Anyone operating, largely or completely, on the primitive brain level that sees another person being ridiculed will have an instinctive reaction. Most will likely be repelled by the idea of siding with the target and will even join in the ridicule. This is a diversionary tactic to promote survival. This behavior reveals low self-esteem. The primitive brain is also responsible for rage.

21:33 Running from the **Truth** is a flight response and patently of the Sinker mindset.

21:34 If one is living centered in the primitive brain mentality it will likely be difficult to gain perspective on personal behavior. **Hate, fear,** and **base contentment** all come out of the primitive brain center. These do not lend vitality to introspection. Uninterrupted introspection focused on the heart will reveal a true and loving understanding of oneself. To the Sinker this will not appear quickly. If truly identified the sentiment will not change over time.

21:35 The **mammalian brain** is the portion of the human brain that propels the Thinker mentality. This part of the brain contains the **frontal lobe** and **cerebral cortex**, among other sections. Mammals have this more complex brain structure in addition to the reptilian section. The mammalian brain in humans controls more evolved mental activities including speech and reason. Other attributes include sophisticated appreciation of art, literature, and culture. At the height of the mammalian brain function humans enter into intellectual realms of abstract thought. The mammalian brain and the Thinker mentality is what have lifted humankind to its dominant position on earth. Reptiles and birds do not possess the more complex mammalian brain structure.

21:36 How one sees themselves is the first order of discerning whether beneficial behavior is being put into practice. The individual is shown to be more inclined to one or the other mindset by their desire to honestly review themselves. One would seek this view to create the most positive environment for themselves and those around them.

This will lead to **personal growth, fulfillment,** and **greater awareness** of purpose and potential. What a person tells him or herself will reveal, at that moment, in that thought, if they are acting predominately as a Thinker or as a Sinker. How much one cares about what they think is indicative as well.

21:37 Gaining perspective on one's level of awareness is a worthy endeavor. The efforts invested in this assignment will pay endless dividends in the form of **love, wisdom,** and **bliss**. If one's thoughts are negatively emotional they are more in line with the Sinker mentality. If one's thoughts are calmly logical they are more in line with the Thinker mentality. Observing one's own behavior objectively over a sustained period of time will point in a consistent direction. Dispassionately acknowledging one's self-discovery can lead to improved and uplifting circumstances in one's life.

21:38 Without gaining full understanding of one's position on the scale of human awareness uplifting behavior may still be implemented. The Power To Love may be applied mechanically leading to Thinker behavior. Disregarding the emotional need to judge in situations that are not life threatening will diminish Sinker tendencies. The Power To Love will focus one's attention on enriching circumstances. If one is engaged in matters that are loving and uplifting, behaviors lacking love, and that are suppressive, will have less influence. Opening one's heart to love will, by definition, exclude one from having a closed heart refusing love.

21:39 This can be done by focusing on what one loves - building up what one loves in place of tearing down something one might not prefer. We perform acts of love or acts lacking love but never both at the same time. Love can overwhelm something that lacks love, but pursuing actions that lack love will never produce love.

Chapter 22
Where We Go From Here
(Skimming the Surface)

22:01 There is only one race
of humans on earth.

22:02 The history of
earth is of oppression.

22:03 Recognizing personal
traits can be a challenging proposition.

22:04 To determine where we
go it is beneficial to
determine where we are.

22:05 Any person will likely
tell you they are accepting.

22:06 The judgmental will look
at their life and react emotionally.

22:07 An acceptor will look at
their life and react logically.

22:08 What anyone does with the
information of this world is up to them.

22:09 Where you go from where
you are is your choice.

22:10 Conditions
constitute humanity.

22:11 We inspire when
we breathe in.

22:12 What we are can be cultivated,
or self-inspired, to our desire.

22:13 Life is constantly
calling for action.

Chapter 22
Where We Go From Here
(Entering the Waters)

- It can be challenging for a person to discover their true self.

- The history of the world is one of division and oppression.

- We cannot avoid life.

- How we choose to act and live our lives is up to us.

Chapter 22
Where We Go From Here
(Deeper Depths)

Legendary film director Frank Capra is credited with saying, "You don't make a good film from a bad script."

22:01 There is only one race of humans on earth. What separates people are their traditions and their perspectives. We can be hopeful or fearful. We can be more accepting or more judgmental. We can want all to be free or we can want to control others. Many know the loving ways of life. Many are confused by feelings of helplessness when they look at the state of human relations. No one person can save the world from strife. No one person can bring justice to the globe. All we truly control is ourselves. Being the individuals we have allowed ourselves to be is how we have come to where we are and only as individuals can we shape the future. That is up to each of us. We can act as individuals because that is what we are in our hearts. If we live from our loving hearts we fulfill our role as human beings. Our most fruitful opportunity is to inspire others to an uplifting way of life. The alternative is no alternative.

22:02 The history of earth is of oppression. A large portion of the population has accepted oppression in its many forms. In the guise of providing for the masses, responsibilities have been displaced and liberty has been denied. This is oppressive. It is important to recognize the idea that because humans have the ability of reason they are placed above governmental bodies. To insure security and tranquility, in this arrangement, laws are made that will not impinge on **life, liberty, property,** and the **pursuit of happiness**. And so everyone is clear on this system, all laws apply to all people equally. That is what makes the founding concepts of the **United States of America** a monumental revelation. (If you have difficulty accepting this notion do the required research to speak knowledgeably on the subject - read the **Declaration of Independence**, the **U.S. Constitution** and the **Federalist** essays, also called the Federalist Papers. **DO NOT** settle for someone else's interpretation. Read and ruminate over these concepts and the implications of these ideals.) The Sinker will quickly harangue how the USA is imperfect. All pursuits of humankind include facets that can appear imperfect. Tearing down does not create. Being judgmental does not bring acceptance. People speak of our imperfection for only one end. That end is to spiritually demoralize us as people (worldwide), the metaphoric killing in the prologue of this manuscript.

22:03   Historians have watched the actions of those who have been given the reigns of authority and those who have stolen them. Rights of the many mean nothing to the Sinker. The propaganda drums drone on to keep the truth from being heard. The thoughtful are being shouted down by the thoughtless. The incrementalism the Sinker mentality employs is their only hope for control. The Thinker believes in **self-awareness, self-dependence,** and **self-realization**. These are not traits all people are born with yet mostly obtainable through thoughtful effort. In viewing any public exchange the Thinker and the Sinker are easily identified. Recognizing those traits in ourselves is a different proposition.

22:04   To determine where we go it is beneficial to determine where we are. But we do not go anywhere as a society, we all go as individuals. Regardless of national, or global order, into the distant future there will be Thinkers and Sinkers. How many and how influential will be determinant factors. Where **WE** go from here is more succinctly asked, **"Where do YOU go from here?"** Since everyone is part Thinker and part Sinker we must determine for ourselves what is acceptable to us. What perspective we have acquired and developed for ourselves will influence us greatly. Yet we can change more directly if we correctly know what we are changing from. Change is ever-present going from low to high, high to low, low to not-so-low, high to not-so-high, high to higher and low to lower. Nothing remains unchanged as we are constantly on the move. How we change can be influenced by us or left unguided to become as it may.

22:05 Ask any person and, most likely, they will tell you they are **accepting**. It is completely unimportant as to what anyone calls themselves. We know the value of being accepting and the pejorative implied in being judgmental. What a person thinks and does will indicate who they are in their heart. If we dispassionately witness our actions we will learn the truth of our nature. We need to ascertain, to the best of our abilities, how our individual mind works. Truth is an anathema to the **rage-filled, arrogant,** and **hopeless** mentality of the Total Sinker.

22:06 **The Sinker will look at their life and react emotionally.** The fretting and wringing of hands over circumstances they do not control reveals their emotionalism. They will have prescriptions for what others must do. The Sinker will focus on organizing authority for themselves behind calls of injustice. Their plan of action will be sweeping changes to consolidate control, using ridicule and fear as motivation. The population will be pummeled to comply, allegedly for the good of all.

22:07 **The Thinker will look at their life and react logically.** Remember a non-action is an action. It is logical to sometimes accept something for what it is, even if it is not desired. Though the Thinker will pursue goals to improve their condition, they will do so with less focus on the negative actions of others. Instead the Thinker will build their dream knowing it is their dream and their right. Accepting the traditions and perspectives of others is reasonable when the innocent are not abusively assaulted. Humans deserve dignity and humane treatment. How a Sinker looks pass their thought process to justify the desire to control is nothing short of astounding. Their espoused belief of a, "live and let live," philosophy can assume many contortions before reason intercedes.

22:08   What anyone does with the information in this book is up to them. **There are no mistakes.** If someone partakes in abusive action they stand in direct confrontation with freedom loving people and will find themselves called upon to explain their actions. This may not occur on the first day of their transgression yet be assured the day is coming. Oppression will not stand forever. Freedom is a natural yearning of thoughtful people. If people act to abdicate their sovereignty others will wrest that authority. When a population properly claims the birthright of humanity to be self-determinant the usurpers will be banished. The Sinker is destine to be discarded. The rewards of thoughtful living are the highest ideals of humanity. Professing the desire for freedom means nothing without the vigilance of action to assure its security.

22:09 A righteous population will not assume a **nationalistic, industrial,** or **spiritual** stance simply because they are told to. Whether looking at their life or being told what to think the Sinker will respond emotionally. How we respond is our choice. Where **YOU** go from here is **YOUR** choice. The Sinker will observe what is around them and emotion will dominate their attention.

22:10 A variety of conditions constitute humanity. In a diverse community or nation there are differing conditions. In a successful community or nation there is a thread that bonds the citizens together. These bonds include **common beliefs, language,** and **culture** shared in the hearts of the citizenry. The common beliefs include that each person is created equal, with unique purpose and abilities, also a belief in the **Rule of Law** created with the **consent of the governed**. The common language is of love and acceptance. And the common culture is a desire for **self-awareness, self-dependence,** and **self-realization**. When we look to ourselves as the gift that we are, we develop ourselves to express the facets that we have come to understand as that gift. We have a duty to guard ourselves from being persuaded into actions that do not benefit us as individuals; actions that are designed to suppress our individuality; actions that promote ideals that discard the individual. We ought to have an allegiance to our individual freedom to be who and what we are, not just for ourselves but also for all who act as individuals.

22:11 There's a medical term for when someone dies. The term is that the person, **"expires."** Sounds like a coupon or an offer of some kind. The offer expires and their life is over. There is another medical term for when someone breathes in or inhales. That term is that the person, **"inspires."** We all remember times when we were thrilled and inspired. Most would say they like being, "inspired." Learning about meditation, the first thing a person is told is to consider their breath. The student is taught in a roundabout way to self-inspire. One of the easiest ways to bring energy into our body is to breathe in. Obviously, the oxygen in the air is needed for muscle and brain function but there is something unseen in the air that is available to us when we, "inspire." That energy is breathed in and delivered to facilitate the flow of our life force, our **Chi**. This Chi can be focused or free flowing. Where this inspiration goes our energy follows.

22:12 What we are can be **cultivated**, or **self-inspired**, to our desire. The alternative to this is to allow ourselves to become whatever our instincts produce within us. Even if one does not know what kind of a Thinker and how much of a Sinker they are there are actions that can be taken to discard the fearful grip of emotionalism. When we engage one behavior the other will diminish. **The Power To Love** reduces less-positive behaviors. By replacing thoughts of **fear, anger, sorrow, remorse, hopelessness,** and **humiliation** with positive thoughts and reinforcing actions we change our world. Being able to do this will show where one is on the scales of **willingness** and **ability**. Understanding this proposition and not engaging self-awareness reveals more of one's own frailties.

22:13 Life consists of highly frequently reoccurring demands upon us to respond to the events in and around us. Remember a non-action is an action. It is not so much important how we feel but that we get to decide how we feel. When we comprehend morality it is incumbent upon us to respond morally. For if we do not, we knowingly undermine our life experience into a downward trend. This opens a path for the Sinker mentality to pull us beneath the surface of the water. If we need to and then choose to not teach ourselves to swim, when we do not swim, we choose to expose ourselves to sinking into a life lacking love.

Thinkers and Sinkers

Epilogue
(Skimming the Surface)

E1:01 Judgment is in a death
match with acceptance.

E1:02 With thoughts and actions
someone judgmental can
become accepting.

E1:03 The ancient Egyptians
understood that happiness or
sadness await after this life.

E1:04 The ancient Greeks learned
of the various levels of the afterlife.

E1:05 Christian teaching reflects
consequences in Heaven and Hell.

E1:06 Judgment has rooted
governments and influences
that destroy lives.

E1:07 When we attempt to
contribute, we will contribute.

E1:08 Utopias are the fantasy of
those who are unrealistic and judgmental.

E1:09 Only once someone learns
can they begin to understand there
is always more to learn.

E1:10 What sets human life
above all other life forms is
our ability to reason.

E1:11 When we give our potential
away, we reject our gift.

E1:12 Thoughtfully consider if
you want to be someone
who loves or hates.

E1:13 One cannot examine their
subconscious, yet one can
program their subconscious.

E1:14 In our thoughts and actions
we direct ourselves toward more
of how we think and act.

Epilogue
(Entering the Waters)

- In the dynamic that is life, there is a tug of war between oppression and liberty, humanity is the rope and the prize yet also the deciding factor.

- For life to have any meaning there must be life after death.

- Judgment is a tool used to stoke fear and manifest control.

- Many will focus on what they do not want, but when we focus on what we want and we attempt to achieve, we find success to some degree.

- We produce nothing when we quit. There is no reason in not trying. We choose if we will try.

- Our habits lead us to what we create, bring into, and experience in our life.

Epilogue
(Deeper Depths)

E1:01 **The Sinker Ideology** is in a death match with its rival . . . **Love**. All of the lessons created by humankind revolve around this one point. The battle between good and evil has so vividly been illustrated throughout time in an attempt to do everything to keep people from getting too close to the edge. This edge is the event horizon where everything that passes over it turns straight down and into the jaws of the Sinker mentality.

E1:02 While we are in physical form we can alter our thoughts and actions to lift ourselves away from this pit of a loveless reality. Once our life ends the body and the spirit part ways. The **body decays** and as the spirit **we continue our journey** elsewhere. Much as in life, our mental disposition directs us toward our continued experience. The destination for those possessed by the Sinker mentality is very likely the less-hopeful environment depicted throughout the ages.

E1:03 The ancient Egyptians taught of a divine character of retribution that consumed the souls of those who poorly lived life. This personage had several titles including; **"Greatness of Death," "Eater of Hearts,"** and **"Devourer of Souls."** Upon the death of the body, the life, in the form of the heart of the deceased, was weighed against Truth. Truth was represented in the form of a feather. If the heart weighed out correctly the deceased would enter into an eternal life with the gods, and all that would bring. If the heart was heavier than the feather, or in some accountings not the same weight as the feather, the heart was devoured. The Egyptian belief was that in life the heart is where the soul resides. When the heart is devoured the soul is consumed. This led to an eternally restless afterlife. This fate excluded the deceased from ever entering the heavenly paradise after death. These eventualities of potential despair or elation are found in other teachings.

E1:04 The ancient Greeks learned of the **Underworld** and the various levels of the afterlife. Less-honorable souls were beset by sorrow, lamentation, and forgetfulness. There was even outright torture due those who were delivered to **Tartarus**, the deepest level of the Underworld. Heroic, virtuous, and initiated souls were favored with comforts and enjoyed perfect happiness in **The Elysian Fields**. As we come forward in history the names change but the sentiments do not.

E1:05 Christian teachings reflect similar consequences of older belief systems. **Heaven** and **Hell** are broadly understood representations of hopeful and less-hopeful circumstances that result from a life lived well and otherwise. But for many their perspectives submit them to consider life to be a hell on earth. They are unwilling or are truly unable to see advantages and opportunities before them. This state-of-mind directs their actions to reinforce that mindset and that reality. Many of these people seek and gain influence over others and whole nations.

E1:06 Viewed from Western Freedoms; **Totalitarianism, Communism, Fascism, Collectivism, Statism, Socialism,** and **Progressivism,** and by extrapolation the Sinker mentality, have been shown to be abject failures - forms of governance and influences that destroy lives. A thoughtful person can explain why. These systems fail for two reasons. First, these systems discard the individual. This is the same as removing one's heart and spirit. This is done to extinguish all drive to achieve, serve others, and love. Second, these systems are designed to fail and to spiritually kill the oppressed. There is no possibility for a loving success in the Total Sinker mentality. If the trend is not reversed the Total Sinker system will continue degrading, pulling all attached down into chaos. The suffering of the oppressed will only last so long. It may take generations but the oppressor will fall in many instances to be replaced with a similarly oppressive force less developed than the previous yet pointed in the same direction.

E1:07   Solutions which place burdens upon the productive to provide for the unwilling to produce are proposed to displace responsibilities. We all have things we cannot do for ourselves. As we respond within our ability to help ourselves and those we can we express the quality of our heart. In so doing we lift those around us and ourselves in ways matching those qualities. This may not be the ultimate effort needed to extricate one's self from the Sinker mindset but the action points the individual away from undermining their own happiness. This is the underlying decision in everything we do.

E1:08   **Utopias** are the fantasy of those who are unrealistic and those who wish to motivate the **unaware**, placate the **useful**, and manipulate the **thoughtless** into line with the Sinker mindset. A utopia is an imagined place or state-of-being where everything is perfect. The word, "utopia" is based on the Greek, **"ou,"** meaning, **"not,"** and, **"topos,"** meaning, **"place."** The word describes somewhere that does not and cannot exist. It is silliness to think there is a place that, for the same reason, can be described by everyone as perfect. This also might be thought to imply that where we are cannot be found to hold perfection for each. This further points up dissatisfaction on the part of some. Judgment points the mind toward dystopias and to disregard the possibilities and potentials of one's surroundings and life.

E1:09   There is a fascinating hypothesis called **The Dunning–Kruger effect**. This hypothesis submits that there is a cognitive bias where people make poor decisions and choices but because they are unaware of their incompetence they are unable to recognize these actions. From there this effect gives them a sense of superiority, which leads to future poor decisions and choices. In their ignorance they believe they are intelligent. The redeeming factor is found in the posit that if these less-competent individuals are taught to greatly increase their abilities they can realize and acknowledge their past lack of competence. This realization should be a humbling experience and when embraced a whole new world will appear before them ready to support the expression of their loving heart.

E1:10 What sets human life above all other life forms on this planet is the ability to reason. The word, **"Logos"** has been interpreted throughout time with evolving meaning. In its essence, Logos combines **thought, words,** and **logic**. Descartes wrote, **"I think, therefore I am."** Why we are here is debated yet as we are here we think. The effort we dedicate to our thought process renders to us understanding, comfort, and reason however well founded. But if we stop thinking we stop evolving. If we stop evolving we begin to devolve. If embraced, this will lead to a dominant Sinker mentality. The hyper-dynamic nature of this world deserves our engagement. Without engaging life we live mundane and thoughtless lives of instinct, lives that conceal paths forward to untold richness of experience and boundless fulfillment of purpose.

E1:11 This book was written to prompt the reader to, deeply and personally, consider their thought process. For each, our lives are about us. When we give our happiness and potential away we reject our gift. When we allow **situations, events,** and **persons** to dictate or otherwise control our experience we cease to live our lives. If we choose to live our lives for ourselves we realize the uplifting nature inherent in **giving, loving,** and **receiving**. If we succumb to judgment we enter our potential into a vast maelstrom to be consumed by **chaos**, the very same chaos from which logos emerged bringing order to this world. These two states are available to us, yet when all is said and done each of us will come to rest in one or the other.

E1:12 If you do nothing else, engage **The Power To Love** in regards to this book. If you love it, great, embrace the concepts shared here. Share this book with your friends. Re-read and study this book often - meditate on the message. What you have learned can pass to others simply by your knowing and acting on the concepts. Visualize how others can benefit from the concepts in this book. If you have a less than favorable reaction to the book be neutral and pass on the concepts offered here. If you feel a visceral response that you are compelled to voice and act out in ways that would tear down this book look at yourself, you are displaying the Sinker mentality. Thoughtfully consider if you want that for yourself and what that will possibly bring to you.

E1:13 What is in our subconscious mind influences us. Think about what is in your subconscious mind . . . **YOU CAN NOT!** It is in your subconscious. You are not able to review what is in your subconscious but you can influence and eventually program what is in your subconscious. By thoughts and actions you create much of the fabric that is your subconscious mind. It has been created and you can only guess as to what is there, yet you can create your subconscious anew, to your liking, consciously.

E1:14 This book dissects and delineates the extremes found in the polar mindset that permeates humanity. Through our thoughts and actions we are each pointed and flowing toward becoming more one than the other of these two mindsets. Suggested in these pages is a simple and deliberate path toward the higher mind of genuine **self-expression, fulfillment,** and **love**. That path is **The Power To Love** (chapter 20). The opposite of which is a dismissal of **individuality, potential,** and **purpose**. Without end we are called upon to direct ourselves to the destination of our choosing. Over time those choices affect us completely through our sense of experience. This experience will direct us to our next experience. That means we will live with consequences in this life and beyond. What we receive is what we ask for. Recognize what you are asking for. It is in your life today.

Epilogue Conclusion

For the foreseeable future the stark influences between judgment and acceptance will likely persist. In these crosscurrents we find every living soul. Yet how these influences persist will be affected by the choices we make in living our lives. These effects have great potential to resonate with us in, and after, this life. Between the two, one, the Sinker, rides over us relentlessly seeking to render us confined, impotent, and unfulfilled. The other, the Thinker, waits eagerly to inspire, support, and uplift. While we are human we are finite . . . nevertheless capable of wondrous things. Directing our attention, directs our connection.

We are blessed with everything we need if we pursue the desires of our loving heart. Yet if our loving heart is not known to us we are lost to our truest desires. The depth of our introspection will guide our thoughts and actions, producing matching works. Our engagement leads to fulfillment. Our actions reveal our thoughts. We can succumb to judgment and promote confusion or we can engage acceptance and promote The Power To Love.

We, and our world, function on many levels. Though we can influence others we also influence ourselves.

If we choose judgment we join the Sinkers. If we choose acceptance we join the Thinkers. Every time we act we choose and influence ourselves and very likely others. If we do not thoughtfully choose how we influence, how we influence will result thoughtlessly unchosen.

What do you want for yourself?

Concordance

"S" = Skimming the Surface, "E" = Entering the Waters,
"D" or unmarked = Deeper Depths, ("E1"= "Complete" Epilogue)

A

aberrant behavior, 03:03

abnormal, 03:02, 03:03, (see: normal)

abundant, 05:09, 07:28, (plentiful, bountiful, available in large quantities)

acceptor, 01:05, 01:08, 01:12, 09:14, 14:06, S 22:07, (The behavior of not judging others, yet not complacent regarding laws and personal convictions.)

accumulation, 05:17, 05:20, 09:03, (In many ways the individual is an accumulation of sorts.)

actor, 10:11, 10:13, 13:12, 18:12, poster in Ch. 20, (The person who acts, activates, engages activity, interacts, reacts, and can include non-actions.)

ageism, 18:13

allowance, S 06:08, S 06:11, D 06:08, 06:11

American Revolution, 15:08

aptus, 21:03, (Latin meaning, "fit"), (see: attitude)

argumentum ad hominem, 02:08

attitude, S 20:07, S 21:03, D 21:03, 21:04, 21:05 (attitude is everything, D 21:03), (see: aptus)

attraction, S 08:05, D 08:04, 08:06, 20:12

authoritative rule, 01:14

authority, 06:12, 07:03, 07:18, 07:20, 11:06, S 12:01, S 12:02, S 12:03, S 12:06, E Ch. 12, D 12:01, 12:05, 12:06, 12:07, E Ch. 17, D 17:06, 22:03, 22:06, 22:08

Awareness Through Reflection, 20:17

B

balance, 01:08, 01:09, 03:30, S 03:31, S 03:33, E Ch. 3, D 06:08, 13:01

belief, 00:03, 01:09, E Ch. 2, D 02:12, 02:14, 02:16, 08:13, 11:17, 12:15, 18:15, 20:28, 22:07, 22:10, E1:03, E1:05

belligerent, E Ch. 10, D 10:01, 10:02, 10:03, 10:05, 10:06,

F

K

kill, 00:02, 01:15, S 10:05, D 10:05, 19:03, 19:07, 19:28, 19:30, 19:33, 21:31, E1:06
killing, 19:06, 22:02

L

leisure, E Ch. 4, D 04:29, 04:29, 04:30, 04:31
less-able swimmer, 08:13, S 14:04
less-capable swimmer, 00:15, 01:13
less-loving, 03:26
liberty, 03:23, poster in Ch. 3, D 07:34, 11:07, S 12:20, D 12:20, 22:02, (liberties, poster in Ch. 20)
Life, Liberty, and Property, S 12:20, D 12:20
Lincoln, Abraham, poster in Ch. 11
lock out, 04:11, 04:14
Logos, E1:10, E1:11
Love for Freedom, Nation, and Morality, 17:13

M

mammalian brain, 21:35
manipulate, 00:01, S 02:08, D 02:04, 02:08, 02:16, 03:28, poster in Ch. 3, D 07:30, 08:16, 18:17, S 19:23, D 19:03, 19:22, E1:08
market forces, 04:21
masculinity, 13:03
media, (the), 04:17
metacognition, 02:11
metaphors, 14:01
micro-behaviors, 18:08
modus operandi, 19:03
molecules, 08:01
morality, 17:13, poster in Ch. 20
murder, S 11:04, D 11:04, 19:09, 19:15, S 20:25, D 20:25, 21:31

N

narcissistic, 07:35
nationality, S 01:02, D 01:02
Natural Law, poster in Ch. 3, D 03:06, 03:07

R

S

V

W

Y

Concordance

About the Author

DAVIDA PATRICK MOORE

The greatest attribute of humankind is that of reason. How one develops insight on spiritual and philosophical matters is often not achieved through academic channels. Davida Patrick Moore has spent nothing less than decades acting, observing, and reflecting upon questions asked since the dawn of humanity and answers long ignored by our collective and dominate ego.

Davida is an uncommon author. Without the required education, standard or otherwise, his being drawn to writing is one of happenstance more than anything else. A well-grounded Catholic grade school education followed by an unenthusiastic public high school education fostered and then reinforced his disinterest in what he found offered to him in the guise of education. During his youth he had been fascinated by the devotees of astrology, meditation, and the Tarot, but much of what he saw felt more like entertainment than a deep and abiding enlightenment.

From 1997 to 2002 Davida provided journalistic, opinion, and entertainment contributions to the production of "ShadowWorld, South Bay Music Scene Magazine & Guide" (South Bay of Los Angeles). He was the publisher and editor, as well as, interviewer, reviewer, production staff, advertisement sales department, distributor, commentary writer, and advice columnist. In those years he also had a weekly column in The Easy Reader Newspaper (Hermosa Beach, CA). By the time he folded his magazine Davida had begun writing spiritual and philosophical essays to share online his years of exploration and experience. Communication of ideas has always appealed to him as the foundation of our intellectual evolution. The writing of "Thinkers and Sinkers," became a two-year endeavor.

Born in 1959 on the West Coast of the United States, Davida has spent most of his life between Seattle, San Francisco, and Los Angeles. In his childhood and early adult years he was awash in the influences of society, the media, and several siblings (younger GenXers and older Baby Boomers). He was presented the chaotic currents of the 1960s and saw the loosening of many from their chosen convictions. The rock music, "British Invasion," and the following hippie explosion amplified this scattering. As time went on, the whirlwind of public discourse was constant as it was repeated that nearly everything was up for questioning. To Davida the 1970s showed little promise of answering the heartfelt questions of society, and the individual. Forces at work, at the time, seemed uncaring. The frenzy of the 1980s resembled the driving of a herd less than the culturing of humanity. This did not abate in the 1990s.

photo by: Blanka Kielb

Davida Patrick Moore

Up until the time of this printing, creeping obfuscation of auspicious American history along with the fanatical rhetoric of strident public voices has done little to convince Davida that all is well understood.

Once in every long-lived life a crystalline moment in time shocks awake the public senses. This moment came again on September 11th, 2001. These catalytic events have always been accompanied by great conflagration. In the history of America these events include; World War II, The American Civil War, and the American Revolutionary War. Belligerent war is difficult to forgive. War of survival is essential. However one feels about the struggle within humanity during the early 21st Century one must recognize that between the opposing sides one is belligerent as the other strives to survive. How one arrives at their personal understanding of this state is a direct reflection of how they conceive of and perceive themselves, others, and the world around them. This is what catapulted Davida Patrick Moore to write and discuss this fractious reasoning. He believes that how we respond will structure how we see our past, live in the present, and determine the range of possibilities for our future. Thoughtfully or thoughtlessly this is how we live life. Through his experience this thought process is brought into focus.

Davida believes the documentation of the main thesis of, "Thinkers and Sinkers," is already found in every person's life. The honesty and introspection needed to honor one's own situation and travails is often difficult to cleanly allow into being. He sees that so many struggle with accepting parameters of life that the lowering of the only protection they know, their ego, is onerous. "Thinkers and Sinkers," is projected through Davida's personal prism and reveals his reasoning. This is done for others to partake of as they might. With sufficient thought it becomes clear most resonate at their core with the same happiness we all seek. Attending to this core is the work of overcoming egocentric behavior and dispatching the fear that holds us in place. These are realities understood by those who have, along with the author, attempted to endeavor this calling.

Following his intuition, Davida Patrick Moore was led to explore communication and behavior. In the course of his life he has discovered, demystified, and embraced a form of personal expression that is best described as bi-gender. The fluidity and appreciable nature of the masculine and feminine allows him more genuine self-expression. Spirituality and philosophy are his natural pursuits and are found in his compositions. Asserting his focus in on humanity, he dismisses calls of intellectualism toward his work. His writings include; music, poetry, lyrics, plays, visual scripts, essays, monologues, and now books. As a life-long musician he most identifies with the classical, jazz, pop, and rock genres. Feeling assured by the sense that he is structured yet freeform in his life he lives in the hope that all people will find and express their true and loving heart.

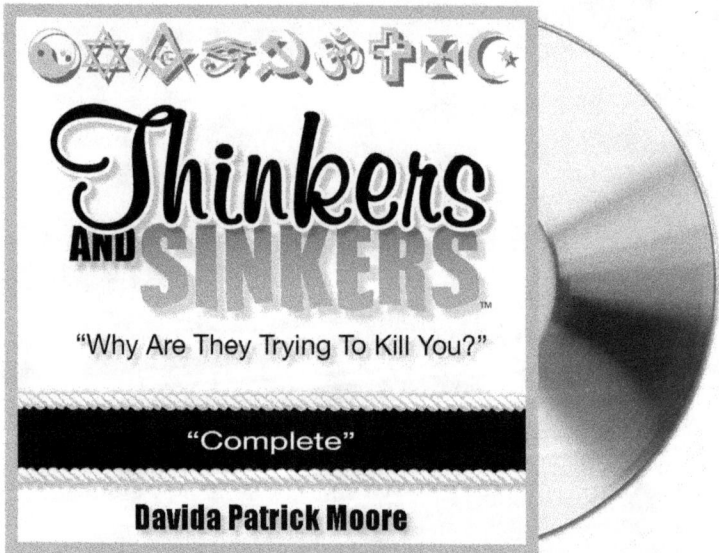

Upon the publishing of this edition of, "Thinkers and Sinkers," this audio recording is offered on a single compact disc in the mp3 format. There are 88 tracks on the CD so the reader can easily begin at a wide range of start points in the text. Notice the audio track number indicator (seen below), these appear throughout the book located at the top of the page where the track begins.

> ⏸)) audio track #001

As technology improves the delivery of this material may be presented in a different format than describe above. Always this material will be offered in what is determined to be the widest available and most flexible format of the day. In the future, this may even include a choice of formats.

The appearance of the packaging for this CD and successive offerings may vary from the representations found on these pages.

Thank you for your interest and for taking the time to study, "Thinkers and Sinkers."

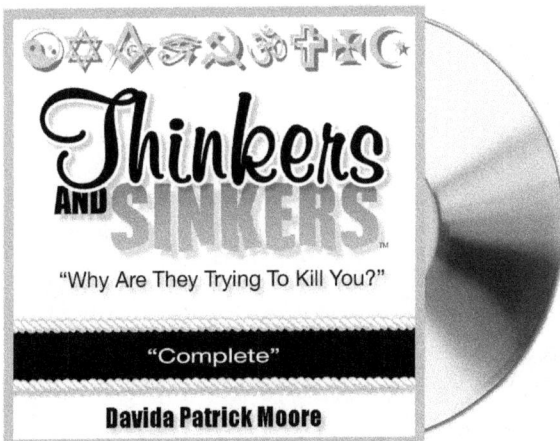

Thinkers
AND SINKERS™
"Why Are They Trying To Kill You?"

"Complete"

Davida Patrick Moore